Defend Yourself with Kung Fu
A Practical Guide

By the same author

Every Boy's Judo
Judo Guide to Black Belt
Defend Yourself With Karate
The Science of Judo
Defend Yourself with Judo

Defend Yourself with Kung Fu

A Practical Guide

A P Harrington

Judo Black Belt 2nd Dan of Kodokan, Tokyo
Brown Belt of Karate

Former Secretary, British Register and Council of Black Belts Association Ltd

Stanley Paul, London

Stanley Paul & Co Ltd
3 Fitzroy Square, London W1

An imprint of the Hutchinson Publishing Group

London Melbourne Sydney Auckland
Wellington Johannesburg Cape Town
and agencies throughout the world

First published 1975

Set in Monotype Baskerville
Printed in Great Britain by The Anchor Press Ltd
and bound by Wm Brendon & Son Ltd
both of Tiptree, Essex

ISBN 0 09 122690 2 (cased)
0 09 122691 0 (paper)

'To cling to the submissive is called strength'

– Lao Tzu.

Acknowledgements

I wish to note my gratitude to my dear wife Lilian, eldest daughter Jane and Linda Chapple for their kind help with the typing of the manuscript and photographs provided for the artist's reference.

Contents

Introduction

I have designed this book for both men and women who have had no previous practical experience of Kung Fu.

While elementary techniques have been described in the following pages, I have been careful to make certain that the style of Kung Fu offered is not limited in its potential scope, and there is no reason why the subject matter should not provide a sound basis for developing future expertise in the art.

There should be no competition whatsoever between you and your helpmate, when practising the recommended techniques which follow, until you both become thoroughly well versed in the art. If you mistakenly do not help one another as much as possible in the early stages of training, it can prove to be a very real hindrance to both of you in your progress in Kung Fu.

In the line illustrations you will notice that the defender is depicted as wearing no jacket. This is because I have tried to show precisely how the upper body should be positioned for the application of each technique.

Kung Fu can be considered as the 'grandfather' of Ju-Jutsu, modern Judo, Aikido and the various forms of Karate now practised throughout the world. While developments over the succeeding centuries have occurred, the basic essentials of the art have apparently remained constant and withstood the ruthless test of an extended time scale.

To my mind, there is a misleading impression among many educated people that activities such as Kung Fu propagate the use of violence. I believe, on the contrary, that training in such fighting arts as Kung Fu actually serve safely to dissipate aggressive tendencies, which appear to me to be inherent in both the young as well as the not so young men. In addition, the strict discipline of training required for both brain and body in acquiring skill in the art tends to increase control over such seemingly natural, but socially disruptive, aggressive tendencies.

A. P. HARRINGTON

LONDON

The Source of Kung Fu

Taoism, one of the three main religious cultures of China, forms the basis of the spiritual reasoning which underlies the physical discipline of the art of Kung Fu.

Throughout the course of its history, extending beyond Christian times, there seem always to have been two main groups who interpreted Taoism in quite different fashions.

The first group, headed by the Celestial Master (T'ien Shih) had their large hereditary estate on the Dragon Tiger Mountain in Kiang-Si province for about 1800 years. Followers of the Celestial Master are the 'Principle One' sect, and these master sorcerers and exorcists obtain diplomas in the magical arts. These wizards or *fang shih* have generally lived and moved freely among the peasants. They marry and hand on their skills – performing magic, telling fortunes and selling charms – to their children. The Celestial Master receives from his predecessor a sacred sword as a mark of his high office. This sacred 'Excalibur-like' sword is viewed by the followers as an instrument of miracle and the Celestial Master is believed to be able to transmit his own hidden powers over nature to his disciples.

The second group, which most concerns us, for the purpose of this book, is composed of monks. Unlike the magicians, they withdraw from society to live in monasteries and adopt a celibate way of life. They follow a sparing vegetarian diet, fasting for purification, and observe complete abstinence from alcohol and tobacco. They practise meditation, breath control and gymnastics, in an attempt to unite the soul with the body, and believe that sickness and disease are the direct result of a transgression of the laws which govern the universe. The monks therefore try to live in harmony with nature, which explains why they do not kill for food.

The early Taoists sought to achieve immortality through their way of life. According to them, if they could keep the yin-yang forces, which they considered to be the opposing forces of which life is composed, in perfect equilibrium, there was no reason why life should not be prolonged indefinitely. When however they realized that death was finally inevitable, they evolved the concept of an inner consciousness which would endure after the death of the physical body. This fundamental change really meant that Taoism then became a religious culture.

The monks adhere very closely to the teachings of Lao Tzu, an older contemporary of Confucius, who set forth moral guidelines for the state as well as the private individual. Lao Tzu gives the key to survival for the individual as humility and gentleness. The principal idea behind his writings is the concept of *Tao* (the way). This term represents, for Confucianists, the way to heaven. To the Taoist, it means this much and more. It is the indefinable and unchangeable energy of being, the eternal life-force which guides and rules over the fate of men. According to Lao Tzu:

> 'It is because he (the sage) does not fight that no one in the world is in a position to fight him.'

Much of Lao Tzu's reasoning appears at first sight to be paradoxical. In Taoist philosophy, the weak will overcome the strong, either by merely remaining passive or by waiting for the opponent to be overcome by someone stronger yet.

'To cling to the submissive is called strength.' In Taoism we must strive to become what Lao Tzu describes as the 'uncarved block', which is the state we reach when we have freedom from worldly ambition, since there is no offence greater in Taoism than having too many desires. We must overcome the senses and the mind in order to achieve contentment.

Posture and Movement

It is vital that the correct stances and postures are practised by you before you even consider the actual technique which follows. Kung Fu has five basic positions for the feet. In Kung Fu these positions are: normal upright posture and the stances of Dragon, Frog, Horse Riding and Snake.

Normal Upright Posture

This stance is static and is one in which you squarely face the opponent. Your feet are kept about shoulder width apart with the weight of your body equally supported between your feet. The body should be kept straight, with legs only slightly bent in order not unduly to restrict any subsequent movement or avoiding action.

Dragon Stance

This stance is very effective in fighting and is probably the most widely used. The stance bears some resemblance to the posture adopted by the majority of Occidental boxers when sparring, although in Kung Fu the feet are firmly planted upon the surface with the forward leg used to support most of the weight of the body.

You firstly adopt the normal upright posture. Step about eighteen inches diagonally to your left on to your left foot so that your left leg becomes well bent, and allow your right leg to become straightened behind you. It is important to ensure that you keep your back straight throughout this shift of position and do not lean forward.

If we visualize the clock-face and take it that you are facing 12, then both of your feet should have the toes pointing to the direction of the hour hand when it is one o'clock. This careful positioning of your feet will permit you to advance or retreat very quickly. Continue by lowering your body weight so that your feet become firmly planted on the surface with the left foot supporting two thirds of your total weight. You should twist your left knee outwards so that your whole posture becomes stabilized. On no account ought you to allow your left knee to become lowered inwards, even though you will find the necessary outward twist which is imparted to your left knee joint to be awkward at the beginning of training.

Position your left fist in front of the left side of your chest and right fist by your right hip with palm uppermost (*Figure 1*).

Now begin to move forward by stepping a small pace with your left foot followed by your right foot. After you

Figure 1

have progressed a few paces forward in this style of movement, reverse the process by moving backwards. Be watchful to see that you do not straighten your body too much during your change of position, as otherwise your feet will tend adversely to have only fleeting contact with the surface. Once you have become acclimatized to moving directly forward and backwards across your practice area, move in every direction possible until you can do this smoothly with equal facility in any direction.

On no account should you skimp over this section of the book, since correct postures form the basis upon which you can build an individual style which, in turn, will enable you to possess a smooth and competent movement pattern.

After you have gained a useful working knowledge of the Dragon Stance with left foot in advance, I recommend you to try out the same type of stance with your right foot in advance. Remember, however, to see that you carefully adopt the correct posture.

Since you cannot always expect to be in a position to advance a foot, you should also adopt the Dragon Stance by moving your right foot diagonally backwards as your left leg is allowed to become bent. Once again also try out the reverse stance, by this time moving your left foot diagonally backwards, as your right leg becomes bent.

Frog Stance

This is a most excellent activity for exercising the skeleton of the body quite apart from the necessity of getting used to adopting a very low stance for Kung Fu.

Stand in the normal upright posture then turn your feet so that your toes point slightly inwards. Your clenched fists should then be positioned by their respective hips, with palms uppermost. Slide your right foot outwards and marginally forward to your right, until your left leg becomes straightened, and then bend your right leg well. If you now imagine a straight line drawn between your feet, the toes of your left foot will be in alignment with the heel of your right foot. Make certain that you do not lean forward from the waist as you lower your body to adopt a firmly balanced, low posture, with your left leg straightened and right leg kept well bent. While the toes of both feet continue to point inwards, your right knee must be twisted outwards. Punch diagonally downwards with your left fist.

Support your body weight upon your right leg as you continue your actions by moving your left foot inwards, close to the inside of your right foot and straightaway outwards again diagonally to your left. Once your left foot becomes replaced upon the ground, with toes pointed inwards, allow your right leg to become straightened and bend your left leg well. Your left knee must be twisted outwards. Retract your left fist to your left hip and punch diagonally downwards with your right fist as you tense your whole body (*Figure 2*).

Figure 2

Continue by firstly moving your right foot inwards until it almost touches your left foot and then outwards again, diagonally to your right. When you replace your right foot on the ground, turn the toes inward and bend your right leg well as you straighten your left leg. Your right knee is now twisted outwards. Ascertain that the toes of your feet stay pointed inwards before continuing your movements by moving your left foot.

The activity just described consists in progressing very slowly, and gradually, forward across your practice area. On no account should you make anything but minute forward and backward progress when taking up this stance, as otherwise the benefits to be derived are minimized. It is a cardinal error to move forward or backward too much when the change of position occurs.

When you prepare to move backwards, you take a foot outwards and slightly backwards before bending the leg and straightening the other leg.

Make certain that you do not proceed further in training until you have acquired a thorough knowledge of the requisite change in position called for when moving forward and backward.

Snake Stance

The basis of this stance is to maintain the majority of one's weight on the rear leg with the advanced leg bearing very little of the body's weight.

Take up the normal upright posture with your feet shoulder width apart and opened left hand forward and opened right hand positioned with little finger edge against your breastbone. Advance your left foot and replace it on the ground some fifteen to eighteen inches in front of its original position. While the whole of your left foot rests quite firmly upon the surface, the majority of your body weight continues to be supported by your right leg. The correct proportion of body weight supported by each leg in this stance is reckoned to be about two-thirds on the bent back leg and approximately one-third on the rather more straightened forward leg (*Figure 3*).

Progress by shifting the major portion of your body weight to your left leg, as it becomes bent, and glide your right foot some fifteen inches forward. At this juncture

Figure 3

your right foot is lightly placed upon the surface in front of you, while your bent left leg maintains the greater proportion of your weight. Reverse the position of your hands by moving your opened right hand forward as you retract your opened left hand to your breastbone.

Once you have become used to the actions called for in this stance, move reasonably quickly forward and backward, and take up the required posture after each step.

Iron Horse Stance

The descriptive name of Iron Horse Stance probably stems from the posture that one adopts, which is very similar to the complete silhouette of a rider's body when astride a horse.

I think that this type of stance was primarily devised for defending oneself when forward or backward movement is found to be impracticable. Also, it is a very strong and formidable static defensive stance. Presumably if one is unlucky enough to be precariously positioned on a narrow ledge and in danger of attack, then this is an ideal stance to take up.

Adopt the normal upright posture. Move your left foot directly to your left, so that it becomes replaced on the ground about a yard away from your right foot. Point the toes of your feet inwards, then bend your legs well. Stabilize your position by twisting your knees outwards. It is vital that your back remains straight and that you do not lean forward (*Figure 4*).

Figure 4

Once you have become used to implementing the stance, progress by moving exactly sideways. Let us presuppose that you will continue to move directly to your left. Supporting the whole of your body weight on your left leg, move your right foot inwards, bypassing the front of your left foot and replace your right foot on the ground, close to the outside of your left foot. Now support your weight momentarily on your right foot, before moving your left foot behind your right foot, a full yard to your left. When your feet once again become spaced widely apart, re-adopt your strong posture with legs bent, feet pointed inward and knees twisted outward. Again move to your left, in the way just described, remembering to keep your back straight.

After you have practised moving to your left, substitute right for left where necessary, so that you move in the same manner to your right.

As you move precisely to your left and right across your practice area, continuously bear in mind the concept of the 'narrow ledge' so that you keep precisely to a limited 'pathway'.

Kung Fu Defensive Fighting

I place the greatest importance on this section of Kung Fu. If an assailant lands even one powerful blow on a vulnerable part of your body, all the knowledge of technique you may possess is then made largely superfluous. It is vital that you assiduously train yourself to respond automatically to any attacking move that may be made against you, so that you block each and every attacking action. Even blows that you may consider gentle should always be properly blocked or avoided.

I have carefully considered the best way to learn Kung Fu. It seems to me most efficient to learn the fighting moves in two ways. Firstly, for the purpose of realism, it is worthwhile to try the moves out with a helpmate. He (or she) must co-operate with you initially by ensuring that there is no competition between you, which shows itself by unexpected or speedy blows, as otherwise the benefits to be derived from training become reduced.

I think there is no real necessity initially to use powerful defensive actions against your partner, as otherwise you may unintentionally bruise him (or her). All that is necessary at first is to obtain a sound understanding of the defensive methods of Kung Fu.

After you have acquired a sound working knowledge in this form of training, it is very beneficial to practise the moves over and over again by oneself. This is termed in Kung Fu as '*tar fong khuen*' – attacking the air. Also sometimes termed as '*moh chau*' – freely translated as sharpening one's claws! This intrinsic part of training in Kung Fu is dealt with later in the book.

After careful consideration, I have decided not to describe more than a few techniques involving the use of the unclenched hand, even though such techniques form a part of the fighting technique of Kung Fu. This is because I think that only after a considerable amount of careful training is it safe to utilize such techniques, due to the otherwise real danger of breaking or damaging the fingers. Since I have placed the emphasis throughout this book on effectiveness coupled with ease of learning, I have decided not to incorporate certain techniques which could prove dangerous to you during early training.

Rising Hand Block (Pah Sau Tonk) against Punch to Face

Stand facing your partner about two full paces apart and both adopt the normal upright posture. Position your right fists, with palm uppermost, by your right hips and left fists, with thumb uppermost, about twelve inches in front of the left side of your chests.

Ask your partner slowly to step forward with his right foot, and then, in slow motion, to move his right fist diagonally upwards, directly toward your nose. As his fist nears your nose, he imparts a twisting action to his wrist, so that the knuckles of his fist become uppermost.

When your partner advances his right foot, withdraw your left foot and take up the Dragon Stance with right leg forward.

Prepare to use the little finger edge of your right wrist slowly and gently to knock his right wrist upward so that his right fist is prevented from reaching your nose. Begin to achieve this blocking action by moving your right fist diagonally upwards, in a punching action, towards a point about six inches in front of your left shoulder. As your fist reaches this point, suddenly twist your right wrist so that the knuckles of your fist twist toward you and the thumb of your right hand becomes twisted toward the ground. Continue moving your right fist diagonally upwards a trifle more so that you safely brush your partner's fist away from your face. Tense the whole of your body as the blocking action is made and momentarily hold your breath (*Figure 5*).

You will have noticed that by the purposeful twisting of your lower right arm your partner's right arm is diverted upwards. This twisting action is performed in the majority of Kung Fu blocking actions. Be careful to see that no speedy or violent movements are used, as otherwise you may bruise your partner's wrist. Indeed, these defensive actions are quite heavy blows in their own right when applied in

Figure 5

earnest. Sometimes a somewhat inexperienced man will wildly attack one, even in training, with a tremendous flurry of feet and fists. Such a man can abruptly be taught a not too drastic cautionary lesson by blocking actions applied to tender parts of his lower arms and legs!

Continue your actions by retracting your right fist to your left hip with palm uppermost, as you slowly move your left fist toward your partner's breastbone in a counter blow. As your left arm becomes straightened, twist your fist so that your knuckles become uppermost just before you brush your knuckles against your partner's breastbone (*Figure 6*).

Figure 6

After you have gone through the motions of delivering the counter-punch with your left fist, exhale and partially relax your body.

Request your partner once more to step forward, upon this occasion with his left foot, as he prepares gently and slowly to punch you on the nose with his left fist. When your partner steps forward with his left foot, take back your right foot a large pace, bypassing the inside of your left foot. Hold your breath then get ready gently to use the outside edge of your left wrist to impel his left wrist upwards so that his light blow becomes deflected upwards. Move your left fist diagonally upwards, from left to right, in front of your right shoulder and then twist your fist so that the thumb of your left hand is nearest the ground. By the implementation of these actions the little finger edge of your left wrist will lightly contact your partner's left wrist which will cause his arm to be knocked upwards. Momentarily tense the whole of your body as you perform the blocking action.

Once you have prevented your partner's left fist from contacting with your nose, retract your left fist to your left hip as you slowly move your right fist toward his breastbone in a counter punch. Remember that as your right fist nears his chest you must twist your fist so that the knuckles become twisted uppermost just before the punch lightly brushes against your partner's chest. Once again tense your whole body momentarily as you make the blow.

When you have completed your counter-punch, exhale but still continue the defence and counter. Do not waste time by moving across your practice space before recommencing, simply both twist about and move to the opposite direction. Also do not disturb the rhythmic movement by offering your partner the chance to try out the defence too soon. It is most important to achieve synchronized timing so that you are both more able to concentrate easily on technique.

It is a common mistake 'to take turns' by accomplishing one technique before letting your partner take his turn by trying out the individual technique. This is a hindrance to you both. You should instead preserve continuity in action by keeping your respective roles for some considerable time.

After you have practised this compound blocking and counter-attacking action you will notice that one fist is retracted to the hip as the other arm moves forward in a counter movement. This type of contrary action ensures that the maximum power can be utilized in serious circumstances. In addition it ensures that one arm, at least, will provide a protective screen against attack.

Outside Block (Ngoi Cheen Sau Tonk) against Punch to Chest

The essence of this blocking action is to knock aside your partner's wrist with the little finger bone edge of your wrist, to prevent him punching you in the chest.

Both you and your partner should face one another about four feet apart, before adopting the Dragon Stance with your left feet in advance.

Request your partner to step forward onto his right foot and slowly make as if to punch you in the breastbone. Synchronize your timing so that you take back your left foot a full pace as your partner advances his right leg. Move your right fist outward and upward until it becomes positioned about twelve inches away from the right side of your head, with the palm twisted outwards and knuckles nearest your head. At this juncture your arm is bent with forearm vertical to the ground. Hold your breath, then swing your right fist, with exaggerated slowness, downward and inward. As your right wrist nears your partner's oncoming right wrist, twist your right fist, so that the palm of your right hand becomes twisted toward you. Tense your whole body as you bring the little finger edge of your right wrist into contact with the thumb edge of his right wrist and thus propel the light movement of his right first directly to your left. Cease the movement of your bent right arm when your right fist comes to be positioned in front of the left side of your chest (*Figure 7*).

After you have swept aside your partner's slow moving right fist, prepare to use the back of your right fist as though to rap against his right cheek. Relax your muscles somewhat, before curving your right fist inwards toward the pulse side of your right wrist and then straighten your right arm and go through the motions of rapping the knuckles of your right fist, by curving the fist outwards toward the back of your right wrist, in a 'back-handed' blow against your partner's right cheekbone (*Figure 8*). You again tense your whole body just prior to making the blow. After making the blow, you should relax and continue breathing normally.

Figure 7

Now ask your partner once again to step forward. He should advance his left leg and make as if to strike you in the breastbone with his left fist. You, for your part, must move your right leg backwards as you retract your right fist, palm uppermost, to your right hip.

After you have taken up your new position, with left leg forward, prepare softly to divert your partner's left arm, by using your left wrist. Hold your breath as you move your left fist diagonally upwards until your left fist is positioned some twelve inches away from the left side of your head, with palm turned outwards and knuckles nearest your head. At this stage the left forearm and wrist of your bent left arm are vertical to the ground. Swing your left fist inwards and downwards, with controlled slowness so that the little finger edge of your left wrist contacts the thumb edge of his left wrist as you tense your whole body, Once your left wrist pushes his left wrist outward, do not make the error of allowing the movement of your left fist to continue beyond the front of the right side of your chest.

Figure 8

Relax fleetingly, then tense your whole body again as you institute your counter-punch by, firstly, curving your left fist toward the pulse side of your left wrist, then secondly, by partially straightening your left arm and flicking your left fist so that you could rap your knuckles against your partner's left cheek bone. After this blow has been made, relax the muscles of your body and re-commence breathing.

Once you have implemented the two compound blocking and counter-attack actions, twist about and continue to try out the compound actions to the opposite direction.

After you have gained a sound knowledge of the actions called for you can, as always, try the counter moves alone in the style of '*tar fong khuen*' which is described in some detail later in the book. When you do this solitary form of training, you imagine that the blocking arm is in turn swung upward and outward, inward and downward and lastly forward.

It is imperative to note that the arm you use for blocking is never permitted by you to go beyond the point necessary safely to deflect an attacker's blow. You must aim to defend an area of about six feet by under two feet. If one of your arms goes outside this protected area, as it were, it will leave you open to counter, and the arm could not be used quickly enough to utilize another defensive technique.

Inside Block (Jiap Cheen Sau Tonk) against Punch to Chest

This technique is also used as a counter to a punch aimed at the chest. Sometimes during the course of a fight, one may be twisted round, partially sideways to the attacker, and there is insufficient time safely to employ an Outside Block (*ngoi cheen sau tonk*). In this event, Inside Block (*jiap cheen sau tonk*) is ideally used. Also in a narrow, confined passageway, it may prove impracticable to move an arm even slightly outwards with which to defend yourself.

Let us assume that you are standing facing your partner about two yards apart. Your partner has his right fist, with thumb uppermost, in front of his chest and left fist positioned, palm uppermost, at his left hip. Your left foot is in advance, your left fist being in front of your chest, with thumb uppermost, and right fist with palm uppermost by your right hip.

Your partner steps forward upon his left foot before delivering a slow moving punch to your breastbone with his left fist. As he moves forward, take your left foot a large pace backwards, bypassing the inside of your right foot, and bend your right leg. Move your right fist to a point close to the front of your left armpit, keeping the knuckles uppermost. Hold your breath as you continue your counter-actions by moving your right fist forward and slightly outwards to your right as you twist the fist so that the palm of the hand becomes turned toward you with the thumb on the right. When this movement causes your bent right arm to be moved forward and outward, it in turn results in the thumb edge of your right wrist being brought gently into contact with the thumb edge of your partner's left wrist, in order to jog his left arm outwards to your right. You tense your whole body as this light contact is made with your partner's arm (*Figure 9*).

Figure 9

Immediately you counter your partner's purposely restricted blow to your chest with your bent right arm you are in a position to deal him a counter-blow by using the same arm. Achieve this by straightening your right arm forward and slightly upwards, as you twist your right fist inwards so that the knuckles become uppermost with thumb positioned on the left. Make as if to punch your partner on the nose with your right fist. Relax and continue breathing normally, as soon as you have gone through the motions of punching him on the nose (*Figure 10*).

Figure 10

Call upon your partner once again to advance. This time he should step forward with his right leg before aiming a gentle punch at your nose with his right fist.

As your partner steps forward upon his right leg, take back your right foot in a large pace and bend your left leg, which thus becomes your advanced leg. Position your left fist near the front of your right armpit while ensuring that the knuckles of your hand are uppermost. Hold your breath and tense your whole body. Implement the blocking action with your bent left arm, by moving your left fist forward and slightly outward to your left, as you twist the fist as that the the palm of your hand becomes turned toward you, with thumb on the left. When the thumb edge of your left fist touches the thumb edge of his right wrist, gently propel his right arm outwards.

Continue your counter-actions by slowly straightening your left arm and twist your left fist inward so that the knuckles become uppermost as your fist nears your partner's nose. Relax your body and release your breath immediately after completing your blow.

Turn about at the completion of the moves just described and continue practising the actions which are called for.

After you have gone back and forth across the practice area available to you, bear in mind that you can also try the moves out by yourself in the style of '*tar fong khuen*'.

Double Handed (Axe Blade) Block (Pek Fu Tau Sau Tonk)

This blocking action is very efficiently used against anyone attempting to grip both of your sleeves or lapels when facing you. The main points to bear in mind are that you must not allow your elbows to be drawn back beyond your sides, and you must make extremely positive actions, in order to regain the initiative which the attacker may initially try to impose upon your actions.

Ask your partner to stand facing you, at a distance of about two paces, and both adopt the normal upright posture stance. Your partner ought to step forward onto his right leg and make as if to grip your opposing sleeves. As your partner advances his right leg, prepare to deflect his arms outwards, by bringing the little finger edge of both wrists into contact with the inside parts of your partner's lower arms (*Figure 11*). Step forward upon your bent right leg.

Hold your breath. Set your counter moves in motion by moving your clenched fists in front of your stomach. Keep your fists close together with the respective little fingers positioned near to one another and palms of hands uppermost. Separate your fists by moving them diagonally upwards and twist them so that the little finger edge of your wrists come gently into contact with the inside parts of your partner's wrists or lower arms. Immediately contact is achieved and you cause your partner's arms to be thrust outwards, dart forward with your feet.

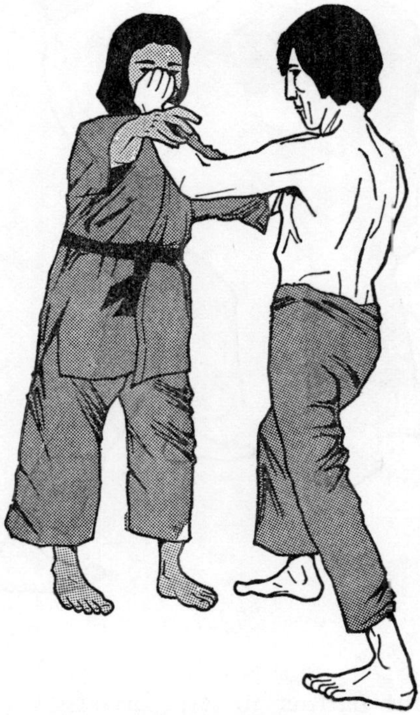

Figure 11

After making this forward move straighten your arms, as you jerk forward from the waist, so that you could make double fisted 'snap' punches to your partner's face (*Figure 12*). Immediately upon going through the motions of the punching action, re-commence breathing and move your upper body backwards so that you regain the upright position.

After you have completed your moves, twist about and

both take a backward pace, so that you are again about two yards apart and facing the opposite direction to the one you faced originally.

Figure 12

Call on your partner to step forward with his left leg before pretending, on this occasion, to grasp your lapels, rather than your sleeves, with his hands.

Start your counter moves by advancing your right leg and move your fists forward in front of your stomach with the little fingers of your hands almost touching. Hold your breath and prepare to tense your whole body. Punch slowly upward and outward with your fists and twist them in order that the little finger edge of your wrists contact the inside parts of your partner's wrists, or lower arms, causing them to be forced apart.

Abruptly jolt forward from the waist and make as if to deliver a double fisted 'snap punch' to your partner's face to finalize your actions. Revert to your upright posture straightaway after delivering the apparent punches. Release your breath and continue breathing normally as you relax your muscles at the completion of your actions.

Palm Block (*Han Sau Pun Tonk*)

In this defensive action you use the flat of your hand, between the base of your fingers and wrist, to knock aside the attacker's oncoming limb.

I have thought it best to give two examples of this defensive action. The first method deals with a punch, while the second deals with a kick.

1ST METHOD

Stand facing your partner about two yards apart and both assume the Dragon Stance with the left foot forward. Your left fists should be positioned about twelve inches in front of the left side of your chests, while the right fists are positioned, palms uppermost, by your right hips.

Your partner ought to make his attack by stepping forward upon his right foot before aiming his right fist slowly, but directly, at your nose.

When your partner steps forward upon his right foot, you step forward and diagonally outwards with your left foot and ensure that your head is inclined to the same direction. Bend your left leg well to make your posture stable, and unclench your left hand while making certain that the straightened fingers and thumb are pressed closely into contact with each other. Hold your breath and get ready to tense your muscles.

As soon as your partner punches forward with his right fist, move the palm of your unclenched left hand from left to right, and gently slap the outside of your partner's lower right arm with the heel of your unclenched left hand, so that his right fist is diverted to your right. It is a necessary safeguard to keep your unclenched hand as rigid as possible and maintain firm contact with his arm from this juncture, until the completion of your counter, so that he could not swing his arm backwards to strike you (*Figure 13*).

Figure 13

Once you have stepped slightly to your left and almost simultaneously deflected the punch, you are ready to counter-attack.

Tightly clench your right hand before twisting your fist so that the knuckles become uppermost as you swing your right elbow forward in a fairly large counter clockwise movement. Gently poke your right elbow into the right side of your partner's lower ribs as your right fist comes near to your own breastbone. When you deliver this blow, ensure that your arm becomes well bent and the whole arm is maintained parallel to the ground, with the knuckles of your fist uppermost (*Figure 14*). Release your breath and re-commence breathing normally as you relax your muscles.

After you have made the retaliating action, both twist about before stepping a pace backward so that you are both ready to resume your actions.

Figure 14

Get your partner to step forward with his left leg and then to make as if to punch you on the nose with his left fist.

As your partner advances his left foot, move your right foot diagonally forward and outward as you move your head and upper body to that direction. Unclench your right hand then press the fingers and thumb firmly into contact with each other. Hold your breath and tense the muscles of your body. Keep your unclenched right hand rigid as you move it first to the right and then to the left, in order that you bring the heel of your hand against your partner's lower left arm unhurriedly, to knock his arm to your left. Strengthen your posture and ensure that your stiffly held right hand continues to press against your partner's left arm. Clench your left fist tightly, then swing your left elbow forward gently into the left side of your partner's ribs as your left fist is brought very close to your breastbone.

Remember not to neglect to practise the movements over and over again.

2ND METHOD

In this method you use the outside part of your palm to deflect the attacker's kicking action aimed at your stomach. In effect the movements described mean that you side step the oncoming foot.

Stand facing one another with the right foot in advance in the Dragon Stance, about two yards away from each other. Your clenched left fists are in front of your chests, with right fists, palm uppermost, at your right hips.

Your partner, for his part, should step forward a full pace upon his left foot, bypassing his right foot, and then he should aim a somewhat tardy kick at your stomach with his right foot.

Your actions call for you initially to withdraw your right foot diagonally backwards behind your left foot as he steps forward with his left foot. Pivot upon your feet as you twist to your right so that you become at right angles to your partner, facing directly to his left. By your purposeful avoiding actions, your partner's right foot will be beginning to pass in front of your left hip, having been prevented from intended contact with your stomach region.

Unclench your left hand and bend your left arm so that your left hand is positioned about six inches away from the outside of your left hip with the palm facing to your left. Ensure that the fingers and thumb of your left hand are pressed tightly together, before your left hand is moved quickly inwards and slightly downwards to your right. Hold your breath and tense the muscles of your body as you twist your left hand into contact with your partner's right calf. As you propel your partner's leg away from your front, slightly twist your hips to your right (*Figure 15*).

Figure 15

In practical experimentation, you will generally find that your moving hand will cause your partner to become partially twisted about to his left.

Once you have evaded the kick and caused your partner to be slightly knocked off balance, you are able to finalize your counter by using a well placed punch to his back or side.

As soon as you have caused his kicking action to veer

harmlessly past your stomach, quickly clench your left hand and retract it to your left hip and make a 'snap' punch with your right fist to your partner's back or side. When you make the punching action, twist your right fist so that the knuckles become uppermost just as your fist nears your partner's back or side.

Release your breath and relax your muscles as you resume normal breathing.

After you have practised using your left hand to divert your partner's right leg, use your right hand against his left leg by substituting left for right where necessary.

Inside Block – with Supporting Fist (*Cheh Lek*)

I have found this ancient blocking action to be very useful in a confined space against a very strong opponent who is known to punch with great force.

The aim of the defender must be to reinforce the arm which is used for the inside blocking action with the fist of the other hand. An additional benefit of which I have become aware when using this technique is that the fist being used to support the blocking arm at the elbow can readily be used to counter attack.

The essence is to learn the technique, from the very beginning, as though you are fighting in what may be quite cramped conditions. I have considered it best, therefore, to constrict the scope of movement advocated in the text so that the blocking actions necessarily become accomplished in a realistic manner.

Request your partner to stand facing you, about four feet away, and both assume the Dragon Stance with left foot in advance. Your left fists are in front of your chests and right fists at your right hips in the accepted way.

Your partner should step forward onto his right foot prior to delivering an intendedly sluggish blow with his right fist aimed directly at your breastbone.

Strengthen your posture by bending your left leg well, then move your left fist to a point just in front of your right armpit. Hold your breath and get ready to tense the muscles of your body. Flick your left fist forward and outwards to your left, with the aim of gently contacting the thumb edge of your partner's moving right wrist with the same edge of your left wrist. Simultaneously reinforce your blocking action by lodging your right fist into position against the inside of your left elbow joint and tense your whole body (*Figure 16*).

Figure 16

Directly after you have employed the double handed blocking action, prepare as though to deliver a straight punch aimed at your partner's right cheek, or nose, with your handily placed right fist. Withdraw your left clenched fist to your left hip, palm uppermost, and contrarily flex your right arm so that the knuckles of your right fist are brought in very close proximity to your partner's right cheek or nose, with the knuckles of your fist now positioned uppermost (*Figure 17*). Relax your muscles and revert to normal breathing.

Figure 17

Continue your training by asking your partner slowly to step forward upon his left leg, after which he should aim his left fist at your breastbone. You start to nullify his attack by taking back your left foot a large pace, by-passing the inside of your right foot, so that your right leg becomes in advance of your left leg. Bend your right leg well and quickly move your right fist near to your left armpit, with thumb closest to your armpit. Hold your breath and get ready to tense your body. Swing your right fist forward and slightly outward to your right and speedily bring your left fist, with palm uppermost, closely against the inside of your right elbow joint, just before the thumb edge of your right wrist contacts with his inner left wrist.

After your unhurried blocking action has pushed aside his left-handed punch, get ready to deliver your counter-punch with your left fist. Flex your left arm and make as if to bring the knuckles of your left hand against his left cheek or his nose. Relax your muscles and renew your normal breathing action.

After you have made the pretence of administering the straight punch to your partner's face, continue by again employing the compound action.

Your partner steps forward with his right foot and punches toward your breastbone with his right fist. Move your right foot a large pace backwards and allow your left leg to become well bent in order firmly to stabilize your position. Hold your breath and tense your whole body. Quickly move your left fist to your right armpit, with palm downwards, then flick your fist forward and outward toward your partner's approaching right fist. As your bent left arm is moving toward your partner's wrist, quickly propel your right fist into contact with the inside of your left elbow, to increase the power of your blocking action. After the thumb edge of your left wrist lightly meets your partner's right wrist, make a straight punch with your right fist. Relax and release your breath.

Upon the completion of the three compound actions, merely turn about and use the moves to the opposite direction. You should both move back and forth across your practice area, in the way described, until you become well versed in the blocking action and counter-punch.

When practising by yourself, use the movements as quickly as possible in order to achieve speed of action.

Rising Crossed Arms Block (*Subji Sau Tonk*)

This blocking action is fitted for use by the defender against a 'Hammer Blow' with a fist aimed at the top of the head, or when the attacker is holding the now notorious 'blunt instrument' of judicial jargon, and tries to bring the weapon downwards upon your head.

To digress a little, it is not wise to use this blocking action when the attacker is holding a knife, or indeed, any sharp pointed weapon. The jarring effect of the blocking movement in forceful action upon the attacker could cause him, voluntarily or otherwise, to release his grip on the weapon. This in turn could cause you to become injured by the pointed end if the weapon were to dart downward upon a vulnerable part of your body. The Palm Block (*han sau pun tonk*) previously described, or Back Palm Block (*sau pun han tonk*), which follows later, are more suitable for countering this type of attack.

Now let us return our attention to Rising Crossed Arms Block. Your defensive aim is to make a scissor-like action with your arms, by crossing them at the wrists, so that the little finger edges of your wrists are used in its blocking position against your partner's downward moving wrist or lower arm.

While adopting the Dragon Stance, both you and your partner should face one another, standing about two yards apart, with your left feet advanced. Get your partner to step forward upon his right leg and then to upraise his right arm before bringing his right fist, with thumb uppermost, downwards upon your head, as though to strike the top of your head with the little-finger edge of his fist.

Your left fist is in front of your chest with right fist tucked close to your right hip. As your partner advances his right leg, bend your left leg well and hold your breath. Thrust your fists diagonally upwards, at an angle of around 45° with the ground and tense your whole body. Your right wrist is made to cross over your left wrist just as you block his right wrist or lower arm with the little-finger edges of your wrists (*Figure 18*).

After you have accomplished the blocking action, make ready to deliver your counter stroke. Unclench your hands and grasp his right sleeve or lower part of his right arm. Bear all of your weight upon your bent left leg, then go through the motions of bringing your right knee into his stomach as you tug him forward to achieve the power of a contrary action (*Figure 19*). Relax and breathe normally.

Figure 18

If the situation warranted it, you could also forcibly use the edge of your shoe against the attacker's shins or ankles after you have used your knee. On the chance that you are barefoot, twist your foot so that the little toe is nearest the ground, and then use the sole of your foot to knock the attacker's leg away from under him.

Once you have performed the defensive action and counter, both turn about and separate into the Dragon Stance, with right foot forward. Carry out the technique by substituting left for right where necessary.

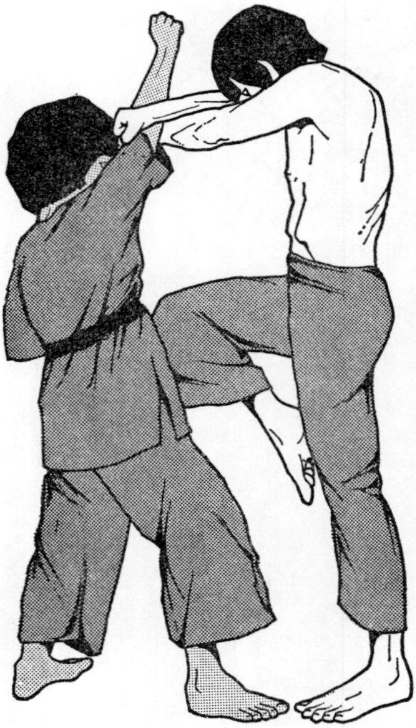

Figure 19

Back Palm Block (*Sau Pun Han Tonk*)

The Back Palm Block is primarily concerned with deflecting, rather than purely blocking, the attacker's blow. For this reason it is especially suitable for the purpose of turning aside the downward blow of an attacker who is clutching a knife, or any sharp, pointed weapon.

Let us assume, as an illustration of a situation in which this tactic may be used to advantage, that your partner is holding a stick aloft in his right hand which he is going to bring straight down on top of your head.

Stand facing each other about two yards apart, with left foot in advance in the Dragon Stance. Keep your left fist forward in front of your chest and right fist, with palm uppermost, at your right hip.

Your partner should initiate the actions by stepping

forward a pace with his right foot, with a stick held aloft in his right hand. He should make the pretence of bringing the stick down on your head. Hold your breath.

As your partner prepares to move the stick downwards, step diagonally forward and outwards upon your bent left leg. Swing your right fist speedily upwards so that the back of your fist is brought into contact with the outside part of his right arm; at the same time, retract your left fist to your left hip, with palm uppermost, and tense your whole body (*Figure 20*).

After you have warded off your partner's right arm, maintain your right arm in position in order to prevent the possibility of your partner momentarily changing his attack by swinging his arm towards you.

Figure 20

Support all of your body weight firmly upon your bent left leg. Raise your right foot up to knee height from the ground and then pretend to kick your partner in the stomach with the toes of your right foot by flicking forward the lower part of your right leg (*Figure 21*). At this time you should relax and assume normal breathing.

Figure 21

Once you have become adroit at implementing the counter with your partner using the stick, holding it in his right hand, ask him to reverse his actions and hold the stick in his left hand.

Both twist about and separate to a distance of about two yards apart. Stand in the Dragon Stance with right foot in advance. Hold your right fist in front of your chest with left fist kept, palm uppermost, at your left hip. Request your partner to step forward onto his left foot and bring the stick downwards toward your head. As your partner upraises the stick in his left hand, step forward and outwards upon your right foot and bend your right leg well. Swing your left fist upwards so that the back of your left fist connects with the outside part of your partner's lower left arm. Keep your left arm in position so as to prevent him from fleetingly stopping your counter moves by varying his attack.

Sustain the whole of your body weight upon your bent right leg and raise your left foot, to knee height, before flicking your lower left leg forward. Retard the movement of your left foot just before contact is made with your partner's stomach.

After you have practised the individual defences just described, against right- and left-handed attacks, get used to defending yourself continuously against the right-sided attack before reverting to the left side. This form of training will, with your partner's kind help, allow you to develop a rhythmic movement.

Knife Hand Block (*Kim Sau Tonk*)

The so-called 'Karate Chop' has now become a hackneyed phrase in our ordinary vocabulary. This one type of blow continues to receive more than its fair share of notice from the media where violence is discussed or depicted.

Generally, it seems the specific blow which is widely depicted as being 'most efficacious' is delivered downwards by the attacker at an angle of 30° to 45° in relation to the ground. Knife Hand Block is calculated to nullify such a blow as the one just described.

Both you and your partner are assumed to be standing facing one another at a distance of about four feet apart, with left foot forward in the Dragon Stance. Your left fist is in front of your chest, while your right fist is kept by your right hip.

Your partner steps forward with his right foot and then brings his unclenched right hand downwards toward the left side of your neck. His supposed intention is to strike your neck with the little finger edge of his right hand.

Unclench your hands, while ensuring that the fingers and thumb of each hand are pressed closely together, so that you do not risk your fingers or thumbs becoming injured in subsequent action.

Move your unclenched hands in front of your chest and cross them at the wrists, with the left hand on top with palm uppermost and right hand with palm downwards. Hold your breath and tense your body. Retract your right hand back toward your breastbone as you sweep your left hand diagonally upwards to meet your partner's oncoming right arm. As your blocking action progresses, impart a twisting action to your left hand so that the little-finger edge lightly glances against the inside part of your partner's lower right arm (*Figure 22*).

Once you have made the blocking action, spread the fingers of your left hand and grasp your partner's right

Figure 22

wrist. Twist his right wrist outwards, by moving your left hand in an anti-clockwise direction, so that the greater portion of his weight is brought to bear upon his right leg, as his upper body becomes tilted to this direction. By twisting your partner's arm in this fashion, you will retard his power of movement, which will be a definite aid in implementing your counter blow. Maintain the pressure upon your partner's right arm as you get ready to direct a counter blow against his body.

If necessary, close the gap between you by stepping quickly forward upon your right foot. Clench your right hand to form a fist and then make as if to deal your partner a blow in the right side of his ribs with your right elbow (*Figure 23*). Revert to normal breathing and relax your body.

Figure 23

Now separate before twisting about so that you may use the technique on the other side when your partner uses his opened left hand against the right side of your neck.

Both take up the Dragon Stance, with right leg in advance, at about four feet distance from one another. Your right fist is in front of your chest and left fist is by your left hip with palm uppermost.

Your partner's actions are to step forward upon his left foot prior to moving his opened left hand gently towards the right side of your neck. Unclench your hands and then bring them in front of your chest. Cross your arms at the wrists so that your right hand is on top with palm facing upwards and left hand has palm downwards. Bend your right leg before swinging your right hand diagonally upwards toward your partner's oncoming left wrist, as you withdraw your left hand to your breastbone. Hold your breath and tense your body as you twist your right hand so that the little-finger edge of your hand contacts your partner's left wrist. As soon as your right hand has impeded the movement of your partner's left wrist, clasp his lower arm and twist his wrist outwards by moving your right hand in a clockwise direction. Your twisting action upon his arm is meant to tilt his upper body somewhat over to his left, so that his left leg is compelled to support the major portion of his body weight. Step forward with your left foot, so that you close with your partner. Clench your left fist and swing your left elbow forward as though sharply to strike the right side of your partner's ribs with the point of your elbow.

As usual, continue to try out the moves together, as many times as possible, so that you become well versed in the performance of the technique.

You can achieve a strong, dynamic blocking action by practising alone in the style of '*tar fong khuen*' – attacking the air.

Downward Block (*Ti Sau Tonk*)

This powerful blocking technique is used to prevent the attacker from kicking the defender in the stomach. It is necessary for the defender to adopt a very low stance in order to gain maximum effectiveness.

You and your partner should stand facing one another, about four feet apart, with left foot forward in the Dragon Stance. Keep your left fist some twelve inches in front of your chest with your right fist held, palm uppermost, at your right hip. For your part, you should keep your feet rather wider apart than usual and bend your left leg well, and thus lower your centre of gravity while allowing your right leg to become extended behind you.

Your partner takes the initiative by kicking slowly forward at your stomach with the toes of his right foot.

Hold your breath. Begin your counter moves by moving your left clenched fist near to your right ear with thumb uppermost and then, without pause, swing your fist diagonally downwards to your left. Just before your fist nears your partner's moving right leg, twist your fist so that the little-finger edge of your left wrist comes slowly into contact with the inside part of your partner's right calf. Tense your body (*Figure 24*).

The blocking action of your left arm will cause your partner's right leg to be knocked outwards and for his convenience he should replace his right foot on the ground, outside your left foot. You must still the movement of your left arm when your left fist reaches a point about six inches above your left knee. The positioning of your blocking arm is important since if you incorrectly allow the movement of your left arm to continue beyond the point above your left knee, you could develop a weakness in technique which would leave you open to counter at a later stage in your training.

In this compound technique, it is best to use what is termed a 'reverse punch' to counter the attacker. This means you use your right fist to deliver a punch to the middle of his body when your left foot is forward, and left fist when your right foot is forward.

Use the punching action of 'reverse punch' against your partner by sharply withdrawing your left fist to your left hip, palm twisted uppermost, as you make a punching

Figure 24

action with your right fist directed at your partner's breastbone. When you make this punching action with your right arm, twist your right fist so that the knuckles become turned uppermost just before light contact is made with your partner's breastbone (*Figure 25*). Relax and go back to normal breathing.

Immediately after you have implemented your punching action, both twist about. Separate to about four feet apart, both facing in the opposite direction from the one you originally faced.

Take up the Dragon Stance with your right fists in front of your chests and left fists held, palms uppermost, by your left hips.

Ask your partner gently to move his left foot towards

your stomach. Bend your right leg well and allow your left leg to become extended behind you, as you adopt a strong position with a lowered centre of gravity. Hold your breath at this juncture.

Move your right fist close to your left ear with thumb kept uppermost. Swing your right fist diagonally downwards

Figure 25

to your right and twist your fist so that the little-finger edge of your right wrist softly connects with the inside part of his left calf. Concurrently tense your whole body. Freeze the outward movement of your right fist, as soon as your fist nears the point about six inches above your right knee. After your right wrist has connected with your partner's left leg he should allow his left foot to land on the ground by the outside of your right foot.

Make as if to implement a 'reverse punch' with your

left fist to your partner's breastbone and twist your fist, so that the knuckles become turned uppermost, just before you deliver a glancing blow. Relax and breathe normally again. Continue to move backward and forward across your practice area until you become adroit in using the necessary actions.

Downward Cross Armed Block (*Sub Jee Sau Luk Tonk*)

The powerful blocking action of Downward Cross Armed Block can be used against the attacker who attempts to kick you in the stomach. It can also be used against the attacker who tries to knee you in the stomach region.

Both you and your partner should face one another about two yards apart before taking up the Dragon Stance with right feet in advance. Your right fists ought to be positioned in front of your chests, while your left fists have their palms uppermost and are close to your left hips.

Let us assume that your partner will step a pace forward onto his left foot, prior to kicking at your stomach with his right foot. You withdraw your right leg as your partner advances.

Continue your actions by adopting a low profile with your left leg well bent. Bring your clenched hands speedily upwards to just in front of your right shoulder. Cross your arms at the wrists so that your right fist is closest to your right shoulder with the backs of your fists in contact with each other. Now hold your breath and tense your whole body. Your next action is to punch diagonally downwards with your fists as you allow a gap of about nine inches to develop between them. You block the approaching right leg of your partner by bringing the little-finger edges of your wrists softly into contact with his right shin (*Figure 26*).

As soon as you have effected the defensive blocking action you are in a position to utilize the counter against your partner. You should uncross your arms as you straighten your arms forward and upwards so that you could deliver double fisted punching actions to your partner's face. Immediately after having figuratively administered your double fisted punches, resume your defensive movements as you relax and breathe normally.

Your partner should shuffle backwards a little to develop a gap of two yards between you. Both take up the Dragon Stance with your left foot in advance. Keep your left fists in front of your chests with your right fists at your right hips with palms uppermost. Ask your partner to step forward a pace onto his right foot, preparatory to moving his left foot slowly forward as though to kick you in the stomach. You move your left leg backwards as he steps forward. Bend your right leg well, to stabilize your posture, and hold your breath. Quickly move your fists close to the front of your left shoulder and cross your arms at the wrists, in such a way that your right fist is nearest your left shoulder. Now punch diagonally downwards to the right and permit

Figure 26

your fists to diverge somewhat so that a gap of around nine inches develops between them. Block your partner's oncoming left leg by moving the little-finger edges of your wrists lightly into contact with the front of his left shin as you tense your whole body.

Upon the execution of your blocking technique you are ready to follow with your counter move. Allow your arms to become uncrossed, as you punch forward with both fists toward your partner's face.

It is important to notice that your punching action requires your arms to be at an approximate angle of 30° to the ground, rather than horizontal as this would otherwise mean you were not strongly balanced with your forward leg well bent.

After you have completed the two compound actions, twist about and try the moves out to the opposite direction.

Punch Block (*Khuen Chooi Tonk*)

When the attacker attempts to punch you in the face with his fist, you can nullify his punching action by the Punch Block. The application of this technique relies on your getting your arm 'inside' that of your partner's when he supposedly attempts to punch you in the face.

It is noteworthy that this is one of the few instances in Kung Fu when a normal punching action is implemented by the defender keeping his arm slightly bent instead of being powerfully straightened.

Both you and your partner assume the Dragon Stance with your left foot and left arm in advance, and right fist at your right hip in the accepted way.

Get your partner to advance his right foot as he prepares to punch you in the face with his right fist. Hold your breath and tense your muscles. Counter your partner by punching toward his face with your left fist, while keeping your left arm slightly bent, so that the outside part of your arm makes contact with the inside of his right arm, and thus prevents his fist from contacting with your face. You will find in practice that provided you keep your left arm slightly bent, the blocking action and punch are effected with hardly a pause in your movements (*Figure 27*). Release your breath at this stage and continue breathing normally as you relax your body.

Figure 27

Your partner ought to follow up his initial punching action with his right fist by stepping forward onto his left foot, prior to aiming his left fist at your face. You move your left foot a large pace backwards as you hold your breath and tense your muscles. Slightly bend your right arm and make as if to punch your partner in the face with your right fist as you impede his left arm by contacting the inside of his left arm with the outside of your right arm. Relax, after having made your right handed punch, and regain your normal breathing rhythm.

Your partner continues his attack now by advancing his right foot as he punches at your face with his right fist. Hold your breath and tense your body. Take your right leg a large pace backwards and slightly bend your left arm, preparatory to punching towards your partner's face with your left fist. Make certain that the outside part of your left arm connects with the inside part of his right arm in order safely to neutralize his punching action. Relax your body and normalize your breathing.

Directly after completing the three separate counters just described, both you and your partner ought to twist about and progress to the opposite direction while carrying out your respective roles of defender and attacker.

Do not be unduly concerned if your 'distancing' is a little awry at the beginning. With co-operation from your helpmate, you will gradually fit into each other's movement pattern so that your timing becomes attuned.

Kick Block (*Wan Tou Keok Tek Tonk*)

It is not always an adequate defence to rely on your hands or arms with which to deflect or block a kick delivered by the attacker below knee height from the ground. In this instance, you can advantageously use your foot to thwart the attack. The object is to make sure that when the attacker viciously kicks forward at your shin, he literally disables himself by smashing his shin forcefully into contact with your aptly positioned shoe or foot.

Both you and your partner stand fully three yards apart, facing each other, with right foot and right arm forward in the Dragon Stance. Your left fists are close to your left hips.

Your partner should step a full pace forward upon his left foot, and then kick with his right foot towards your right shin. As your partner's right foot begins to move slowly towards the lower part of your right leg, you must act. Pivot outwards to the left upon the ball of your left foot until you are sideways to your partner, with your right side nearest him. Bring the sole of your right foot, with toes pointed to your left, softly into contact with the front of your partner's right ankle (*Figure 28*).

Figure 28

It is important to notice that your right foot is positioned horizontally to the ground, with toes pointed directly to your left, when the supposed counter is made. This tactic would ensure that you are afforded a wider margin of error at speed by utilizing the whole length of your foot, rather than merely the width.

As soon as you have completed the counter, back away from your partner, to a distance of about two yards, then ask him to step forward upon his right foot before starting to kick you in the shin with the toes of his left foot. You should have your left foot in advance for this particular exercise. Pivot outwards on the ball of your right foot so that you twist sideways to your partner with your left side nearest him. Raise your left foot and make sure that it is horizontal to the ground, with toes pointed directly to your right, then position your left foot directly in line with your partner's approaching left shin.

Once again back away from your partner to about two yards distance, with your right foot in advance. Ask your partner to step forward upon his left foot, prior to kicking at your right shin with the toes of his right foot. Twist to your left on the ball of your left foot, until your right side is nearest your partner, then position the sole of your right foot in line with his approaching right shin.

After you have gained some considerable training in this technique, you will be able to gain a fraction of advance warning by observing the foot with which the attacker intends to kick, by the preparatory shifting of his weight to the other leg.

Inside Kick Block (*Mai Peen Keok Tek Tonk*)

This blocking action is primarily used when one is adopting the Iron Horse Stance. It seems to me that the further supposition is that the defender is held, and unable to use either of his arms to defend himself from the third attacker, who aims a kick from the front against his groin.

In a predicament of the nature just described, a defender would possibly suffer a bruised leg when forced to use this blocking technique. This would, however, undoubtedly be preferable to sustaining hurt to what is one of the most vulnerable parts of the body.

Aside from the defensive value of this blocking action, it is a valuable form of exercise for developing elasticity in the knee joints, which proves helpful to one's own kicking actions.

Take up the Iron Horse Stance with your feet spread widely apart, with toes inward and knees twisted outward in the way previously described in the section dealing with stances. Ask your partner to stand facing you at some two yards distance with his right foot in front of his left. For his part he should step a full pace forward upon his left foot before carefully bringing his right foot slowly upwards between your legs as though to kick your groin.

You defend yourself by momentarily supporting your weight upon your bent left leg as you flick your right foot inwards and upwards so that your foot glances lightly into contact with the inside of your upper left thigh (*Figure 29*). Your right leg becomes almost fully bent by this kicking

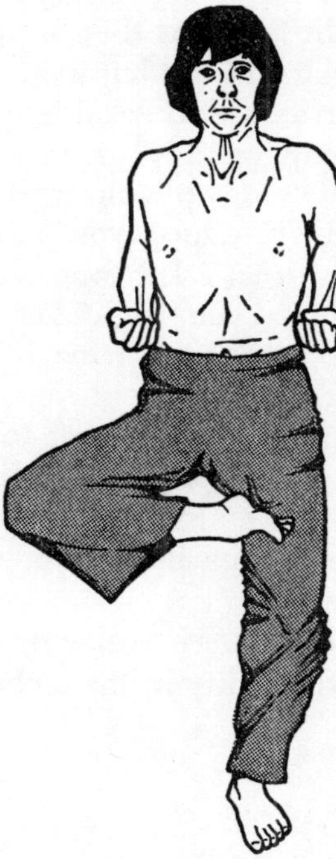

Figure 29

action, and your right lower leg is thus inserted between your partner's advancing foot and your groin. After flicking your right leg inwards in a 'snap-kick' you immediately replace your right foot back to its original place upon the ground, and evenly distribute your weight again on both feet.

You apparently counter your partner in turn by pretending to kick him in the stomach with your right foot.

Make the counter stroke by raising your right foot from the ground, as your right leg becomes bent, then flick your right foot forward into close proximity with his stomach. Tense your whole body momentarily and hold your breath as you perform your retaliatory kicking action.

Your partner should now back away somewhat until he is again some two yards away, but upon this occasion his left foot is in advance of his right. Ask him to step forward a pace upon his right foot and then supposedly aim a kick at your lower stomach with his left foot.

Prevent your partner from kicking you by supporting your weight fleetingly upon your bent right leg as you flick your left foot inward and upward into contact with your inner right thigh. Once you have completed this latter action, your partner's left foot becomes impeded by your right calf. Replace your right foot on the ground as soon as you have blocked your partner's left foot.

Raise your left foot in front of you, so that your left leg becomes bent, then flick your left foot forward so that you make the pretence of striking his stomach with the toes of your left foot. Remember to tense your body and hold your breath momentarily, as you make the kicking action.

Continuously practise the movements together, as usual, in order to gain useful ability in the technique.

Countering Dangerous Attacks

I consider it imperative that we should generally understand the law of England regarding defending yourself against unprovoked physical attack by another person or persons. While the laws of other countries may differ to some extent, the following observations will serve as a general guide.

I believe it correct to assert that it is only lawful for you to use the barest minimum amount of force considered necessary to protect yourself from really serious physical hurt. On no account is it proper or lawful for you, subsequent to an affray, to proffer the excuse of causing injury to another or even others, merely by pleading that you were defending yourself against unwarranted attack. This basis of definition applies to practically any contingency arising outside your own home.

If you are protecting your wife or family from extreme danger in the confines of your own home and expel burglars, or any unlawful intruders, from your premises, then to my mind you are both morally, and I believe legally, entitled to use the amount of force necessary so to do.

In essence, I think the motives for attack against a man generally seem to stem from the two emotions of greed or anger.

It is not always possible to avoid using physical means to resist aggression but, nevertheless, there is very often forewarning of a potentially dangerous situation, if only one could cultivate sufficient awareness of it.

The ancient story is told of three acknowledged masters of the fighting arts who were tested for their ability by a nobleman who required one man to undertake a hazardous and long journey.

The careful test set was that each of the three men was

separately to be invited to walk into the dignatory's private chambers through a door, left slightly ajar, upon the top of which a stick had been balanced. The first aspirant was invited by a servant to walk forward through the doorway, and as he pushed the door open, the stick fell. In a flash he had drawn his sword and cut the stick in half before it had reached halfway to the floor. He was complimented upon his superb skill and ushered into an adjoining room to await the nobleman's summons.

After the stick had been replaced with another, the second aspirant was later ushered toward the slightly opened door. As this man pushed the door open, the stick fell, and he reacted like lightning and caught this stick, before it had fallen but a few inches, with his other hand. He too was complemented upon his great ability and shown to a separate adjoining room. The stick was replaced in its position over the door.

The last man was then brought towards the partially opened door and invited to enter. At this request he smilingly remarked that the great personage must be jesting with a humble man such as he. He went up to the door and carefully removed the stick which he gave to the servant who had accompanied him.

The three men were later called to an audience with the nobleman, where he was to make his choice known. Indicating the first man who had cut the stick in two, he said that while he obviously possessed great skill in the fighting arts, the stick had not posed any real threat, and it was therefore unnecessary to cut the object in two. Acknowledging the second aspirant who had caught the stick, he said he admired this man's great skill and forebearance in not using unnecessary force. Turning to the third man, he said that his great mastery of the fighting arts had obviously transcended the physical, and he wished therefore to appoint him as his choice for the dangerous journey to the far north of the country.

Back Kick (*Hau Pui Sut Tau Koh Keok Tek*)

This kicking action is meant to be used when the standing assailant approaches you from behind, perhaps in a dark place, when he is intent on taking you unawares. He can either be armed with the so-called 'cosh', or intend to grab you from behind as a prelude to further assault.

The great asset of this particular counter technique is that it is not requisite wholly to twist about, to face in the direction of what is perhaps an unexpected attack from behind, with consequent loss of precious time for adequate defensive reaction.

Ask your partner to stand some three yards behind you with a stick or similar object held aloft in his right hand. His actions are to step two full paces forward, first with his left foot, then with his right, with the feigned intention of bringing the stick down on your head.

Start your defensive actions by contorting your hips sharply to your right, so that you twist your right side towards your advancing partner. You can upraise your bent right arm behind you, and then above your head in a defensive warding-off position. Support your weight upon your left leg and raise your right foot from the ground; bend your right leg so that your right knee is positioned in front of your right hip.

Hold your breath and tense your body as you now make a kicking action with your right foot, by flexing your right leg. The toes of your right foot are pointed towards the same direction to which you have purposely twisted in order that your foot is parallel to the ground. The whole length of your foot is used to deliver an apparent kick to your partner's mid-body. Lean forward from the waist just as you implement the kick, to facilitate a reasonably high kick from the ground, and also to move your head as much as possible out of the range of the stick (*Figure 30*).

After you have practised using your right leg with which to kick, use your left leg. Your partner holds the stick in his left hand. He takes up his position about three yards behind you before advancing right foot, left foot, and then presumably trying to bring the stick down upon your head. You twist your hips sharply to your left, so that your left side becomes nearest to your partner. Upraise your bent left arm behind you so that it is above your head in a precautionary warding-off position. Raise your left foot from the

Figure 30

ground until your left knee is poised in front of your left hip. You now ensure that the toes of your left foot point towards the same direction to which you have twisted, with foot parallel to the ground. Flex your left leg, as you lean forward from the waist, so that you could kick your partner in the middle of his body with your left foot.

Once you become adept at utilizing the kick, get your partner to advance more quickly. Remember, however, to judge your kicking actions carefully so that you do not unintentionally make contact, but get used to judging exactly the distance separating you from your partner.

Side Thrust Kick (*Peen Yank Keok Tek*)

In this illustration, you defend yourself from an attack from the side.

You may well find it rather difficult in the initial stages to raise the leg which does the kicking action sufficiently high. It is important that you endeavour, nonetheless, to ensure that during the final stage of the kick, the active leg is positioned horizontally to and parallel to the ground. This would enhance the effectiveness of your counter kick if you were involved in a dangerous situation.

Request your partner to stand some two yards away from your right side with a stick or 'cosh' held aloft in his right hand. He should intend to close with you by stepping forward with his right foot, before bring the stick or 'cosh' down toward your head.

You begin to counter your partner by transferring your weight to your left leg and raising your right foot from the ground until your right knee is in line with your right hip. Twist your left foot slightly outwards. Flex your right leg so that the sole of your right foot is moved sideways to your right, with toes pointed forward, towards your partner's stomach. Still the movement of your right leg just before your foot contacts your partner's stomach (*Figure 31*). Immediately after you have accomplished the kicking action, replace your right foot in its original position upon the ground.

Get your partner to approach you from the direction of your left side. As he approaches to within two yards distance, support your whole weight upon your right leg and raise your left foot from the ground until your left knee is poised in front of your left hip. Straighten your left leg in order that your left foot may become moved sideways to your left. Twist your right foot slightly outwards to your right to facilitate your kicking action.

You can practise this kicking action advantageously

by yourself, but it is recommendable that you do not attempt too many repetitions in too short a space of time; otherwise your legs will possibly tend to become stiff until you become well versed in the requisite action.

Figure 31

After you have become used to implementing Side Thrust Kick directly to your right and left, you should also perform the kicking action directly to your front. Request your partner to stand facing you about two yards away with a stick held aloft in his right hand.

In this defensive action, you should endeavour to regain the initiative by making a positive counter. Step forward upon your left foot before twisting outwards upon your left foot so that your right side becomes twisted toward your partner. Upraise your right foot and when your right knee is in line with your right hip, prepare to make the retaliatory kicking action. Ascertain that the toes of your right foot point directly to your left as you flex your right leg so that the sole of your foot could be brought into contact with your partner's stomach.

You can also use your left leg to make the kicking action by substituting left for right where necessary.

After you have practised some kicking actions to the front, it is wise also to incorporate a variation of Rising Hand Block (*pah sau tonk*) as a future precautionary, self-protective measure for guarding your upper body and head.

Side Flick Kick (Wat Sat Tau Koh Keok Tek)

This technique is fitted for use against attackers who are closing with you from both your right and left side.

You do not necessarily require a helpmate for practising this technique. Adopt the Iron Horse Stance with your legs well bent and spaced widely apart, and toes pointed inwards. Your knees are twisted outwards as you sink downwards into the powerful stance of the Iron Horse.

Position your clenched hands in front of your body. Prepare to make a kick with your right foot to your right. Start your counter moves by stepping inwards with your left foot until it passes closely over the front of your right foot. Place the ball of your left foot on the ground very close to the outside of your right foot, and then hold your breath. Supporting your body weight on your left foot, swing your right foot in a counter-clockwise action around your left foot then flick your right foot upwards toward your right (*Figure 32*).

Your right foot should reach head height before you quickly replace it upon the ground some four feet away from the inside of your left foot and once again adopt the Iron Horse Stance. Release your breath and return to your established breathing action.

You should now get ready to move to your left and use your left foot to flick upwards to your left. Step inwards with your right foot, going over the front of your left foot, and place the ball of your right foot upon the ground just

Figure 32

outside your left foot. Maintain your weight on your right leg and swing your left foot about your right foot, in a clockwise motion. Hold your breath and flick your left foot upwards to your left, to head height.

Immediately after you have completed the kicking action, return your left foot to the ground, some four feet away from the inside of your right foot, and quickly assume the Iron Horse Stance again. Release your breath and regain your normal breathing rhythm as you partially relax your body.

Once you have become used to moving directly to your right and left, while making the kicking actions, gradually speed up your movements until you can move quickly to both directions and assume the Iron Horse Stance immediately after each kicking action. Later still in your training programme, make two consecutive kicking actions to both directions.

Bear in mind the concept of being attacked when precariously placed upon a narrow ledge, or footpath, so that you necessarily move precisely sideways throughout your continuing changes of position; you must also make certain that you quickly keep stabilizing your position in turn, by adopting the Iron Horse Stance. On no account should you twist your upper body sideways too much during your defensive actions.

You will have noticed from the explanations, that you should train by tucking the foot with which you are going to kick behind your other foot. This will make certain that you learn the kicking action in the recognized way.

Stamping Kick (Tit Keok Thum Tek)

This technique can be usefully employed against attackers who are pinioning both of your arms at the sides of your body.

Your first aim ought to be to create a small gap between yourself and the attacker at your right side, who may well be very closely pressed against you and be restricting your power of movement. Wrench yourself away to your left as though to pull the attacker to this direction. When he reacts by pulling you towards him, suddenly reverse your movement by using your right shoulder to barge the attacker away slightly to the right. As your purposeful actions make the attacker recoil somewhat, you are able to use the Stamping Kick against him. Bend your right leg as you raise your right foot from the ground until your right knee is in front of your right hip. Hold your breath and tense your body. (The illustration merely shosw one attacker for clarification.)

Now stamp downwards and diagonally outwards so that you drive the sole of your right foot against his nearest leg between knee and ankle. Concurrently with your stamping kick, you pull this attacker into the kick, by wrenching your right arm once again towards your right side (*Figure 33*).

Figure 33

As soon as you have made the kicking action with your right leg, prepare to deal with the attacker, who is assumed to be tightly clasping your left arm. Exhale and re-establish normal breathing. Again use the attacker's reactions against him by pulling your left arm towards your right, and then quickly use your left shoulder with which to barge him in the chest, as he forcibly reacts by tugging you back toward him. Your counter can be implemented once this stratagem has created a gap between you.

Raise your left foot from the ground as you bend your left leg well, until your left knee is positioned in line with your left hip. Hold your breath and tense your body. Stamp downwards, and slightly outwards, with your left foot so that the sole of your foot is driven into the nearest leg of your attacker, about mid-way between knee and ankle. You do not allow him to minimize your kicking action by moving away, but instead pull him towards you through the medium of his grips upon your left arm. Relax and re-generate your normal breathing activity.

When you get used to performing the compound counter movement in slow motion, really move in a hurly-burly kind of way about your practice area. The more movement you create, the easier will it be to implement the stamping kicks.

From the outset you must not permit yourself to be restricted in a static position, as otherwise you may be placed at some disadvantage.

In reality, you would probably find that the restrictive grips upon your arms would be somewhat relaxed after your stamping actions had taken effect. This would lead to your being able to free your arms from the reduced encumbrance of your attacker's grips. At this stage it is likely that you could satisfactorily implement Side Thrust Kick (*peen yank keok tek*) to both sides in order to knock the attacker's away, and you could then follow with other counters if necessary.

The stamping kick can also be used against the individual who clasps you, either over or under your arms, about the body from the front.

You can achieve this form of defensive kicking action by raising your right foot from the ground before twisting your right foot outwards so that the toes point almost directly to your right. Lean forward from the waist as you stamp downwards and forwards while holding your breath and tensing your whole body. The aim of your stamping action is that the inside edge of your foot or shoe could be scraped down the left shin of the attacker, and then the heel jabbed into his left instep.

It may be useful to grasp the front of the attacker's jacket to prevent his alleviating the power of your stamping action. As usual, you can use your other foot to implement the counter by substituting left for right where needful.

Probable follow-up counters which you could use include elbow blows, back-handed fist blows and Front Kick (*cheen keck tek*).

Round House Kick (*Leng Sun Tek*)

This type of counter-attack kicking action defeats defensive moves which aim solely at protecting the front of the body. The aim is to start the attacking foot in almost a semi-circular movement, so that the kick is delivered from the side of the attacker's body.

It is necessary to master the angle of the retaliatory kicking action as otherwise the skilled attacker may quickly counter your intended move with a blocking action, before resuming his attack.

Your partner can help you achieve the correct direction of attack during the early stages, if he adopts the poses of either Outside Block (*ngoi cheen sau tonk*) or Inside Block (*jiap cheen sau tonk*) as you perform the kicking action. Apart from helping you, your partner will gain useful practice in adopting the required blocking actions.

Take up the Dragon Stance with your left foot in advance of your right. Raise your right foot from the ground and keep your right leg bent, so that your leg is positioned horizontally to the ground, with the inside part of your leg nearest the ground. Continue by pivoting partially around on the ball of your left foot in an anti-clockwise direction to your left and hold your breath. As you twist slightly to your left, flick your right foot forward in an anti-clockwise movement, so that the toes of your foot come lightly into contact with the left side of his back and tense your muscles (*Figure 34*).

After you have seemingly administered the kick with your right foot you must immediately return your right foot to its original place upon the ground. Revert to normal breathing and relax your body.

Figure 34

Ask your partner to retreat two full paces as you advance your right foot past your left, so that you take up the Dragon Stance with your right leg in advance of your left.

Prepare to make the kicking motion with your left leg. Raise your left foot from the ground so that your bent left leg is positioned parallel to the ground, with the inside part of your left leg nearest the surface. Hold your breath and tense your body. Twist partially to your right upon the ball of your right foot, in a clockwise direction, as you flick the lower part of your left leg forward, also in a clockwise direction. When the toes of your left foot lightly glance against the right side of your partner's back, still the movement of your foot. Quickly return your left foot to its starting position upon the ground and relax while resuming normal breathing.

Again ask your partner to move two backward paces away from you as you step forward with your left leg bypassing the inside of your right foot.

Once you have resumed your original Dragon Stance, with left foot in advance, get ready to deliver your third kicking action by using your right foot once more. Raise your right foot from the ground in order that your right leg is bent with the inside part nearest the surface. Tense your body and hold your breath. Twist somewhat to your left on the ball of your left foot, in an anti-clockwise action, as though to kick your partner in the left side of his back with the toes of your right foot. As soon as you have fleetingly contacted your partner's left side with your right foot, return your foot quickly to the ground. At the finalization of these movements you relax and resume normal breathing.

Once you have completed the three kicking motions numerous times, as though advancing, also try the requisite actions while retreating. It is best still to use the three actions in the somewhat halting way advocated, in order that you become thoroughly used to the technique and gain fluidity of movement through repetition.

Front Kick (Cheen Keck Tek)

Front Kick is a most effective counter to an attacker who rushes at you with a club held aloft in his hand. Another example is that if your arms are held from each side by two attackers and a third member of the gang approaches you from the front, you can deliver the effective Front Kick. There are basically two types of Front Kick. In one technique the 'back' leg is used to make the kicking action while in the other technique the 'front' leg is used. The rearward leg is often used for kicking when an opponent has one leg in advance of the other and I consider this a most useful counter. Nonetheless, when the forward leg is also used to implement a kicking action it can also be very disconcerting to the attacker, since it is at closer range, and not such an obviously large movement is called for as when using the back leg.

Stand facing your partner some two yards apart and take up the Dragon Stance with your left foot in advance. Get ready, as though to kick your partner in the middle of his body with your right foot. Tense your body and hold your breath. Bring your right knee forward and upward until it is in front of your stomach; flex your right leg by flicking your lower leg forward. Ascertain that the toes of your right foot lightly contact the front of your partner's stomach (*Figure 35*). As soon as you have made the kicking motion, quickly replace your right foot upon the ground directly below the point of contact with your partner. Relax and go back to normal breathing.

Figure 35

Ask your partner to move back a pace after you have taken up the Dragon Stance with your left foot positioned in advance. Prepare to use your left foot with which to kick your partner while continuously supporting your weight upon your right leg. Hold your breath. Raise your left foot from the ground until your left knee is in front of your stomach. Tense your body then flick your left foot forward as you flex your left leg so that the toes of your left foot glance gently against your partner's stomach (*Figure 36*).

Figure 36

Directly you have flicked your left foot forward and made light contact with your partner, return your foot to the ground in its original position. Relax and resume breathing.

Request your partner to back away three full paces so as to permit you to reverse your leg actions. Step forward with your right leg so that you are in Dragon Stance with right foot forward. Move your left knee forward and upward until your knee is in front of your stomach, then flex your left leg so as to brush your partner's stomach with the toes of your left foot. Immediately return your left foot to its original position.

Follow up your counter-attack by using your advanced right leg to effect the kicking action. Support your body weight solely upon your bent left leg throughout the following actions. Raise your right knee in front of your stomach, then flick your right foot forward so that the back of your right foot glances against your partner's stomach as you tense your body and hold your breath. Immediately replace your right foot upon the ground and relax as you breathe normally.

Move continuously backwards and forwards across your practice area while trying out the counter kicking actions. I think that when kicking with the so-called 'back' leg one is generally regaining the initiative by moving forward, whereas when using the 'front' leg with which to kick the attacker, you are often afforded the chance to deal the attacker a first-rate sneak blow while retreating.

Attacking the Air (Tar Fong Khuen) – or Sharpening the Claws (Moh Chau)

I believe it correct, at present, to observe that a physical action can only become spontaneous when the impulse from brain to limb has been transmitted many thousands of times, so that the path taken by the message becomes well travelled.

Once you accomplish Kung Fu moves without deliberating their component actions, then they are as second nature to you, and you can be sure of being well versed in the art.

You will notice that the particular set of twenty-two techniques described later will entail your using defensive and attacking moves in rapid succession and to all directions of the compass. This training is calculated to provide you with an all round defensive and counter-attacking ability to all directions, so that the potential scope of your expertise in the art is not prematurely limited. Your aim should be to train both your brain and body to function harmoniously when carrying out various fighting actions. I think the whole emphasis should constantly be placed on using maximum effort, and that you should perform the technique using your maximum strength from the earliest possible moment in training.

The principal error to avoid is to believe that after practising a particular series of fighting actions for a short time this is sufficient to provide expertise, or even a useful knowledge.

I believe that centuries ago some of the basic sets of

fighting moves were continuously practised for two or three years by practitioners of the fighting art. With this in mind I urge you not to be impatient or perhaps misled into thinking that constant repetition is not worthwhile. On the contrary, this very repetition, provided it is generally along the right path, is vital to the acclimatization of the body to accomplishing powerful physical actions, and that of the brain to transmitting the requisite diverse and speedy messages for the adoption of the exact fighting poses.

Serenity and patience are the two main virtues developed by thorough training in *tar fong khuen*, quite apart from the considerable physical advantages to be gained.

The story is told of two masters of the fighting arts, who were arguing in a friendly manner, as to who was the most skilful in action. After a seemingly endless discussion, one of them suggested that there was a certain way to prove who was most skilful, and the other willingly agreed to a test of skill.

The man who suggested the idea said that the test would be to tap a monkey on the head with a fan in a large room stacked with chinaware and ornaments. The only conditions being that no harm should come to the monkey and no breakage should occur to the fragile objects in the room. At this ridiculous sounding suggestion, the other said that he always knew his acquaintance to be a mad fellow who thought more than he should. At last, thinking to humour the challenger, and being sure of his superior speed and skill, he agreed to the test.

The room was made ready and the monkey quietly brought in with a little fruit to eat. The challenger said that his acquaintance could enter the room first and attempt to tap the monkey on the head with the fan provided.

The other sneeringly agreed, and stealthily entering the room through the open door, he picked up the fan. He immediately approached the monkey and made as if to tap the creature on the head, with the fan and at great speed. The monkey, thoroughly alarmed, reacted with greater speed to this aggressive movement and leapt away from the intruder. Undaunted, the man hurled himself at the monkey, and in so doing, lurched into several ornaments which shattered under the impact. In a rage he rushed out of the room saying the test was impossible of success, while throwing the fan at the challenger's feet.

Not offering any comment on his acquaintance's outburst, the other picked up the fan, entered the room and sat quietly down on the floor with the fan on his lap. At first the monkey cowered in the corner, but after some minutes, when he saw the man made no move towards him, he became curious and approached the man. The latter still made no move and the monkey came even closer, being deceptively lulled into complacency by the lack of movement from the man. The man continued to sit quite still and patient until the monkey became even bolder, and then very suddenly, he tapped the monkey on the head with the fan. The monkey blinked in surprise and before he had a chance to collect his wits enough to move, the man had lightly tapped him again with the fan. The man then left the room and as he passed his companion, he tapped him on the head, which added to the latter's chagrin.

It is essential that each training session in '*tar fong khuen*' be approached with the knowledge of what you are aiming to achieve. Here are certain precepts which must constantly be kept in mind; they are not necessarily listed in order of importance.

1. *Breathing*. It is essential that the correct timing in breathing be achieved in order that the body can obtain sufficient oxygen to enable the powerful and most tiring actions to be properly accomplished. The recommended time for the inhalation and exhalation of air will be incorporated in the text.

At this juncture in your training you should now be ready to concentrate on correctly breathing very deeply. Imagine that when you breathe in you firstly fill your abdomen with air, as you expand your diaphragm, and then fill the whole of your thorax by expanding your lungs. Do not try to hurry things if it takes a little while to acclimatize yourself to the increased oxygen gained by your body.

2. *Fighting spirit.* One object of this form of training is to familiarize yourself with fighting moves, so that you develop fighting spirit and are not overawed when faced by an unexpected and unwarranted physical attack.

3. *Variation in speed.* The importance of varying your speed of action and reaction to attack and defence ought to be noted. You should gradually gain, through training, the ability to go from a reasonably slow movement to a very fast action in the blink of an eye.

4. *Posture.* The correct posture for each of the fighting poses must be assumed at speed and only constant repetition will ensure that you do not adopt a weak posture.

5. *Development of power.* The acquisition of greater power in defence and counter attack is gradually developed by '*tar fong khuen*' so that the whole strength of the body becomes utilized. After some time spent in correct training you will find your whole actions becoming much more powerful. It is significant to note that even after twenty-seven years spent in practising Judo and other martial arts, I have found the power of my body to have become more than doubled by only a relatively few years' training in '*tar fong khuen*'.

6. *Memory.* The quite involved movement pattern called for when practising a set series of something over twenty defensive and counter-attack moves does develop the attribute of 'instant recall', which is useful when facing a dangerous form of attack.

7. *Focus of power.* Whenever you block or hit you must focus the whole of your attention and power momentarily on the point of apparent contact with the attacker, as you hold your breath and tense your whole body. You will probably notice the intentness which the expert gives to his actions; this is apparent even in a photograph of a skilled man in action.

There are probably hundreds of different 'sets', comprising between twenty to forty techniques, that one could study in the system of *tar fong khuen*. I do not think it possible, unless one was prepared to spend a lifetime in study, to acquire expertise in any but a few 'sets' of technique.

I have found it useful, when first familiarizing myself with a series of techniques, constantly to visualize them in sequence, so that it aids memory when the series actually become performed. By this learning aid, I have mentally pictured a rather involved series of set moves in less than a minute. If during the course of a day this mental 'run through', as it were, is made five times, only five minutes is used, and after a few days it proves most beneficial in training.

Wherever you select your training to take place for *tar fong khuen* it is best always to start facing the same direction. This measure will avoid the complications which might otherwise arise over changes in direction. On this account, if you imagine the compass, you should begin by taking it that the direction to which you are initially facing is always due NORTH. Let us use the directions of the compass in the text to describe the direction to which you turn to face as the series of moves progresses.

To summarize: if you are in a room, the wall you start by facing is NORTH. The wall behind your back is SOUTH. The wall at your left side is WEST. The wall at your right side is EAST. The corner of the room to your left front is NORTH WEST. The corner to your right front is NORTH EAST. The corner to your left rear is SOUTH WEST and the corner to your right rear is SOUTH EAST. In my view, these eight directions will provide all-round protection. The minor directions practically merge with one or other of the eight to which we shall give our attention.

Important note. For explanatory purposes, I have considered also depicting the figures in the illustrations which follow as facing to a particular accepted direction on the page. I decided against this idea since I think it would have necessarily obscured the exact posture of the body which you should adopt for each particular pose.

Preliminary

You start by facing due NORTH with your feet about shoulder width apart and clenched fists by the side of your body. Slide your left foot forward and adopt the Dragon Stance. Now position your left fist in front of the left side of your chest and your right fist, palm uppermost, at your right hip.

1st Movement – Inside Block (Juap Cheen Sau Tonk) – to West

Now prepare to turn in an anti-clockwise direction, exactly to your left so that you come to face WEST.

The assumption is that you are attacked from the WEST with a right-handed punch to your chest region which you counter with Inside Block (*juap cheen sau tonk*).

Twist to your left and withdraw your left foot diagonally backward as you turn to this direction. Bend your left leg well, then move your left fist, keeping your knuckles uppermost, close to your right armpit. Hold your breath and tense your muscles as you flick your left fist forward and slightly outwards, so that the palm of your hand becomes twisted toward you and the thumb is positioned on the left. You still the movement of your arm as you imagine the inside thumb edge of your left wrist has knocked aside the blow (*Figure 37*).

Continue facing WEST.

2nd to 4th Movement – Three Punches – to West

Perform the following three punching actions while continuing to hold your breath and tensing your body whole.

Retract your left fist with palm uppermost to your left hip. Concurrently make a head high punch with your right fist and twist the lower arm so that the knuckles of your fist become uppermost just as you strike the imaginary attacker's nose; the angle of your arm in relation to the ground should

Figure 37

be around 30° (*Figure 38*). Without pause, punch forward at stomach level with your left fist, while in concert with this movement withdraw your right fist, with palm uppermost, to your right hip. Make your third punching action by punching forward chest high with your right fist, as you twist the knuckles uppermost and withdraw your left fist, palm upwards, to your left hip. Exhale and inhale deeply.

The presumption now is that another attacker will attempt to kick you in the back from the EAST and this will impel you to make a rapid clockwise 'right about turn' from the WEST to face this new direction of attack.

5th Movement – Downward Block (Ti Sau Tonk) – to East

Move your right fist backwards over your left shoulder so that your knuckles are uppermost, with thumb close to your

Figure 38

left ear. Hold your breath. Twist to your right and withdraw your right foot a small pace inwards as you swivel on the ball of your left foot so that you smoothly twist through 180° in a clockwise 'right about turn' to face EAST. You immediately stabilize your posture by bending your right leg well, and make a Downward Block *(ti sau tonk)* with your right arm by swinging your right arm diagonally downwards so that you would knock this attacker's lower leg aside with the little-finger edge of your right wrist. The movement of your right fist must cease when it reaches the point about six inches above your right knee *(Figure 39)*. Exhale and then inhale deeply.

Figure 39

6th Movement – Hammer Blow – to East

You continue to face the direction of EAST. The attacker is now assumed to be holding the lower part of your right sleeve or your wrist with one of his hands, after you have accomplished Downward Block *(ti sau tonk)*. You hold your breath as you move your right foot backwards a trifle, so that you become more upright as you wrench the lower part of your right arm diagonally upwards to your left, so that your right fist moves over the point of your left shoulder. After you have apparently wrenched your right arm away from the encumbrance of the attacker's hold, you deal him a Hammer Blow with your right fist. You achieve this counter by swinging your fist upward and then downward toward a point about fifteen inches directly in front of your chest

(Figure 40). At the completion of this blow the thumb of your clenched right fist is uppermost and you imagine that you have used the little-finger edge of your fist to strike at his left collarbone. The movement of your fist is stilled when your right arm is parallel to the ground. You continue facing EAST and resume normal breathing.

Figure 40

7th Movement – Side Thrust Kick (Peen Yank Keok Tek) – to East

You now perform Side Thrust Kick *(peen yank keok tek)* to the direction of EAST to finalize your moves against this same attacker. Move your left foot a pace to your left towards the direction of WEST so that you would create a largish gap between yourself and the attacker and twist your upper body to your left so that you face NORTH. Hold your breath and tense your body. Upraise your bent right leg until your knee is at hip height then flex your leg to your right so that you can make Side Thrust Kick *(peen yank keok tek)* to the direction of EAST with toes of your right foot pointing to NORTH *(Figure 41)*.

Figure 41

8th Movement – Knife Hand Block (Kim Sau Tonk) – to North

Another attacker supposedly tries to 'chop' you in the left side of your neck with the edge of his right hand. You are facing NORTH and you step a tiny pace forward to this direction with your left foot and unclench your hands as you hold your breath. Use your unclenched left hand to make Knife Hand Block by sweeping the little-finger edge of your left hand forward and outwards as though to contact the inside of the attacker's right wrist to prevent the blow from landing on the left side of your neck. Concurrent with your blocking action your right hand is twisted so that your palm becomes uppermost and the little-finger edge of your hand pressed against your breastbone *(Figure 42)*.

Continue to face NORTH as you exhale and inhale.

Figure 42

9th Movement – Front Kick (Cheen Keok Tek) – to North

You still face NORTH. Maintain your weight solely upon your right leg as you bend your left leg and raise your left knee level with your left hip, before flicking the toes of your left foot forward. The kicking action is meant to direct a kick at the middle of this attacker's body. As the kick is made you hold your breath and tense your whole body *(Figure 43)*.

You are now attacked from the direction of EAST.

Figure 43

10th Movement – Back Handed Blow and Side Flick Kick (Wat Sat Tau Koh Keok Tek) – to East

You continue to face NORTH. Exhale as you replace your left foot on the ground close to your right foot and stand perfectly upright. Concurrently form your hands into fists and bring your left fist back to your left hip, palm uppermost, and then press the little-finger edge of your right fist on top of the palm of your left fist. Slightly bend your legs then hold your breath. Flick your right fist upwards and outwards past the front of your right shoulder. Concurrently flick your right foot upwards to your right. Your right foot should reach about chest height with your right fist apparently delivering a back handed blow about face height to this attacker from the direction of EAST *(Figure 44)*. Release your breath and re-commence breathing normally.

You are now attacked from the direction of SOUTH.

Figure 44

11th Movement – Outside Block (Ngoi Cheen Sau Tonk) – to South

Another attacker attacks you from the direction of SOUTH with a right handed punch to your chest. Replace your right foot back on the ground and adopt a rather wide stance while still facing NORTH. You step backwards and inwards with your right foot in a clockwise direction as you pivot inwards on the ball of your left foot so that you twist about to your right to face SOUTH. At the same time you swing your bent right arm to your right until the palm of your right fist is positioned some nine inches away from your right shoulder with thumb nearest your shoulder. Inhale deeply then hold your breath as you bend your right leg well – which should be in front of your left – in order to stabilize your posture. Swing your bent right arm forward and inward so that you would prevent this presumed attacker's original intention to punch you with his right fist. Still the movement of your bent right arm when your right fist nears a point about nine inches in front of your left shoulder *(Figure 45)*. After performing Outside Block *(ngoi cheen sau tonk)* you momentarily relax and resume normal breathing.

You continue facing the direction of SOUTH.

Figure 45

12th Movement – Downward Block (Ti Sau Tonk) – to South

The blocking action of Outside Block (*ngoi cheen sau tonk*) just made by you, will mean that your bent right arm would be inside this attacker's right arm. He immediately attacks you with a left-handed punch aimed at your lower stomach or groin, which you prevent by using a version of Downward Block (*ti sau tonk*) with your right arm. Hold your breath and tense your body, as you move your right fist diagonally downwards toward your right thigh so that the little-finger edge of your right wrist would contact the thumb edge of his left wrist. The movement of your right fist is stilled before it continues beyond the outside of your right thigh. Relax and exhale then inhale immediately and hold your breath. Tense your whole body.

You continue facing SOUTH.

13th Movement – Rising Elbow Blow – to South

You now counter this same attacker from the direction of SOUTH by delivering a Rising Elbow Blow to his chin with your left elbow by swinging your left elbow upwards in front of you. You imagine that you strike this attacker's chin with the point of your left elbow, and still the movement when your left fist nears your left ear with palm of the fist closest to your ear (*Figure 46*). Exhale and take one deep breath as you momentarily relax.

You are now attacked from the direction of SOUTH WEST.

14th Movement – Palm Block (Han Sau Pun Tonk) – to South West

This attacker tries to kick you in the right thigh or stomach from the direction of SOUTH WEST. You twist slightly to your right as you retract your left fist to your left hip and move your right foot outwards to your right to face precisely SOUTH WEST. Hold your breath and tense your body. Swing your unclenched right hand quickly toward the front of your left shoulder with palm uppermost,

Figure 46

before swinging your hand diagonally downwards. You twist your palm inwards and then outwards as your right hand moves to a point about nine inches above your right thigh after 'palming' aside this attacker's lower leg to prevent his left-footed kick (*Figure 47*). Exhale, inhale and then again hold your breath.

You continue facing SOUTH WEST.

15th Movement – Punch to Nose – to South West

You now retaliate against this attacker with a punch to his nose. Tense your whole body as you punch powerfully forward with yout left fist directly to his nose as you retract your right hand, in the form of a fist, to your right hip

Figure 47

(*Figure 48*). Exhale and take a deep breath as you relax momentarily.

An attack develops from the NORTH EAST.

16th Movement – Rising Hand Block (*Pah Sau Tonk*) *– to North East*

This attacker advances from the NORTH EAST as though to punch you in the head with his left fist. You pivot around to your left in an anti-clockwise direction, through 180°, on the balls of your feet. As you make this counter-clockwise turn you swing your extended left arm round in front of you, keeping the arm in the same relative position. Your turning action becomes completed when you come precisely to face NORTH EAST.

Figure 48

At this juncture your left leg is in advance of your right. Hold your breath and tense your muscles. You retract your left fist to your left hip, palm uppermost, and make Rising Hand Block (*pah sau tonk*) with your bent right arm (*Figure 49*). Do this blocking action by keeping your right arm slightly bent as you punch diagonally upwards with your right fist so that the little-finger edge of your right wrist would contact the inside of this attacker's left wrist to knock his blow upwards. Relax fleetingly and exhale then inhale.

You continue facing NORTH EAST.

17th Movement – Punch to Chest – to North East

Once you have made the blocking action with your bent right arm you retract your right fist to your right hip and prepare to punch this attacker in the chest with your left fist. Tense your body and hold your breath. Punch forward with your left fist and twist your fist so that the knuckles

Figure 49

become uppermost just as your arm becomes straightened. Imagine you are punching at chest level. Exhale and take a deep breath.

An attacker now approaches you from the NORTH WEST.

18th Movement – Downward Block (Ti Sau Tonk) – to North West

This attacker moves toward your left side as though to kick you with his right foot. Hold your breath and tense your muscles. You pivot on the balls of your feet to twist to your left. to the direction of NORTH WEST and make Downward Block (*ti sau tonk*) with your left arm. The aim is to ward off this attacker's right foot by contacting his calf with the little finger edge of your left wrist (*Figure 50*). Release your breath then take a deep breath straightaway before again holding your breath.

You continue facing NORTH WEST.

Figure 50

19th Movement – Punch to Nose – to North West

Immediately after effecting Downward Block you stay facing NORTH WEST. Punch forward and upwards with your right fist and twist your right arm just as your arm becomes extended so that you punch the attacker on his nose (*Figure* 51.) Relax as you inhale and then exhale.

The final attacker approaches from the SOUTH EAST.

Figure 51

20th Movement – Downward Block (Ti Sau Tonk) – to South East

This attacker approaches from the SOUTH EAST intending to kick you in the back with his right foot. Hold your breath as you move your right fist over your left shoulder with knuckles uppermost and bring the thumb of your hand close to your left ear (*Figure 52*). Twist speedily about to your right, on the balls of your feet through 180°, and when you come to face SOUTH EAST you tense your muscles and accomplish Downward Block (*ti sau tonk*). Achieve the blocking action by swinging your straightened right arm diagonally downwards as though to knock aside this attacker's oncoming right foot, by contacting the outside of his right calf with the little finger edge of your right wrist. The movement of your arm is frozen when your right fist comes just above your right knee in the accepted position.

You continue facing SOUTH EAST and do not relax.

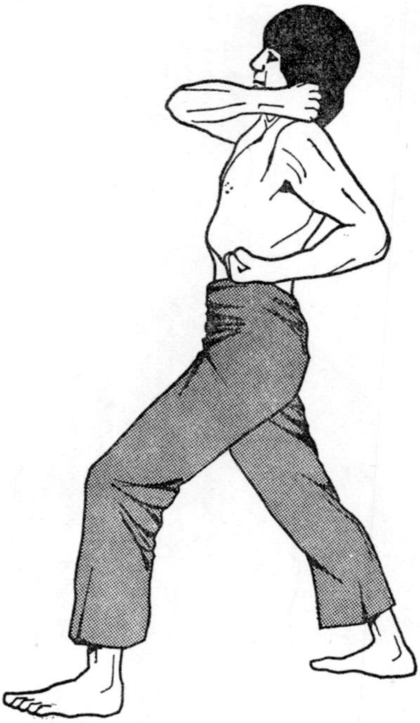

Figure 52

21st Movement – Short Punch to Ribs – to South East

You continue facing the SOUTH EAST. You now counter this final attacker by making a fore-shortened punch with your left fist directed at his ribs. You jab your left fist forward and twist your fist so that the knuckles become uppermost when your left arm is not fully straightened as you retract your right fist to your right hip (*Figure 53*). Exhale and then continue to breathe normally.

Your moves become completed by your pivoting around to face your original starting position of NORTH when you stand with your feet shoulder width apart. Swing your arms forward and upwards in order that they become crossed at

Figure 53

the wrists and then swing your arms diagonally downwards so that your clenched fists come down to their respective sides.

As I observed earlier, you should run quickly through the moves over and over again until you become adept in their performance.

Kung Fu Fighting Technique

22 Techniques

Since the art of Kung Fu embraces the use of many parts of the body, for defence and counter-attack, it is not practical in one volume adequately to cover the many thousands of techniques one could use in fighting against the attacker. I have therefore thought it best, in this section of the book, mainly to concentrate on only some techniques with which to illustrate the different spheres of the Kung Fu fighting technique, so that you may acquire a useful basic knowledge.

Even knowledge of one solitary technique is not to be considered of no use. I was told of a famous exploit, witnessed by a perceptive man, which occurred many years ago, involving a countryman and two champion fighters. The countryman was visiting the city and went along to the largest and most widely respected training centre in the city, where all the most famous fighting masters congregated to demonstrate and test their masterly skills.

The countryman asked permission to take part in the activities and, after watching for a little while, he asked an acknowledged champion if he could test his skill against him – one successful technique to decide the winner. The champion, thinking to humour the rustic, smilingly agreed, and watched by his admirers, walked to the contest area. After they had saluted each other, they came together, whereupon in a flash the countryman had heavily tripped the champion to the ground, flat upon his back, with a throwing technique taught to beginners in the first month of training.

Such an unexpected result caused a tremendous stir amongst the spectators, and the champion demanded the test of skill should continue; but the countryman firmly maintained that it had been agreed in advance that one technique was sufficient to decide the winner.

The countryman then retired quietly to a place in the corner of the spectators' area and sat down. After a couple of hours, and as the afternoon wore on, the constant to-ing and fro-ing of contestants and spectators had resulted in a new crowd of participants and watchers, who took no interest in the unknown man sitting silently alone in the corner – steadfastly watched only by my intrigued informant. The countryman again politely asked the recognizably greatest champion present to a contest and made the same stipulation of one successful technique to decide the winner. Utterly confident of his ability to deal summarily with such an apparent yokel, this champion also agreed to the bout. In the blink of an eye he too had suffered, what was for him, the indignity of being dumped upon his back by a replica of the beginner's technique which had disposed of the other champion.

The countryman then unobtrusively left the scene, presumably to return to his far-off village, leaving behind in the city two very chastened champions.

1st Technique

Stand facing your partner, about twenty-four inches apart, both with your left foot in advance of right in the Dragon Stance. Both of you should position your fists so that the left fist is some twelve inches in front of the chest while the right fist is positioned close to the right side of the chest. This is the basic sparring position which I will use in the explanations.

Your apparent aim is now to convey the impression to your partner that you will attempt a fairly high level counter-attack toward his face. Move both of your fists diagonally upwards as you raise yourself up to your full height. Still the movement of your left fist almost as soon as you begin to deliver a 'snap' punch with your right fist to your partner's face.

Your partner should move his arms upwards to prevent your supposedly punching his face.

Now reverse the movement of your body by stepping diagonally forward with your right foot to your partner's right side so that you adopt a semi-crouching posture. Hold your breath and get ready to tense your body as you make the following action. Straighten your right arm directly outwards to your right before swinging your extended arm backward and then quickly forward so that the inside thumb edge of your lower right arm could be used horizontally to strike the front of your partner's body (*Figure 54*).

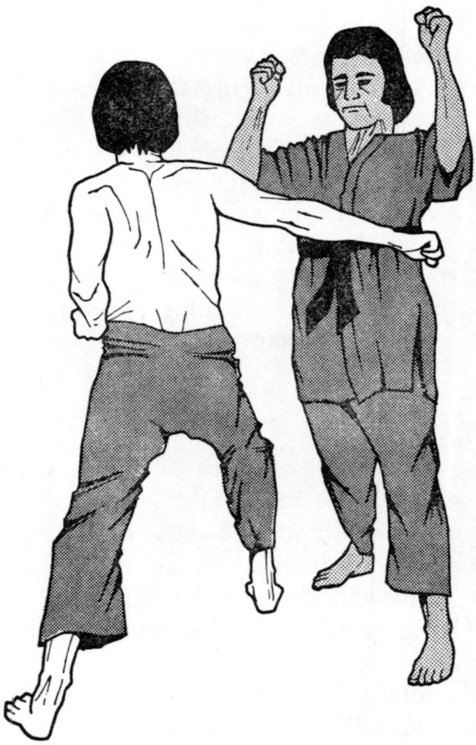

Figure 54

After the inside of your right arm has supposedly been used to strike your partner use the following combination technique.

Bend your right arm and bring your right fist, with knuckles uppermost, close to your left hip. Flick your right fist upwards to your right so that it goes over your partner's right shoulder in order that you could rap the knuckles of your hand against the right side of his face in a back-handed blow (*Figure 55*). Relax and renew your regular breathing action.

Figure 55

After you have practised using your right arm and fist with which to implement the technique many times, switch your actions and use your left arm and fist.

Both you and your partner should again face one another, about two feet apart, while adopting Dragon Stance with right foot in advance of left. Position your right fists about twelve inches in front of your chest while the left fist is positioned close to the left side of your chest.

Raise yourself to your full height while pretending to punch your partner suddenly in the face with your right fist. You pretend to make a 'snap' punch by momentarily moving your fists forward and upwards. Your partner should upraise his arms to block your punch – as he would probably do in reality when attempting to combat this ruse.

Lower your level of attack by stepping diagonally forward upon your bent left leg to your partner's left side. Hold your breath. Stretch your left arm directly outwards to your left and then swing your arm quickly backwards and then forwards, so that you could strike your partner with the thumb edge of your lower left arm as you tense your body. Straightaway after having made as if to strike your partner with your left arm, bend the arm and bring your left fist close to your right hip with knuckles uppermost. Flick your left fist upwards and then over your partner's left shoulder so that you could rap the knuckles of your fist against the left side of his face. Relax and re-institute your usual breathing.

You ought to practise diligently closing with your partner both to left and right so that your different angles of counter-attack are blended together as quickly as possible.

In the example just described your aim would be to obtain a reaction from the attacker so that he would leave himself open to your intended combination counter blows. We are generally inclined, from an early age, to resist force of any shape or kind. This almost inherent resistance to force is even usefully employed against the would-be attacker. If the force you retaliate with is quite dramatically sudden and quite novel in the attacker's experience, then the chances are that his reaction will not be governed by conditioned reflexes acquired through previous experience, but by an uncontrolled response which will generally leave him open to your counter moves.

2nd Technique

In this technique you make a high level counter-attack followed by a low level attack with the same fist.

Both stand facing one another, some twenty-four inches apart, with right foot in advance while adopting Dragon Stance. Your right fists should be positioned some twelve inches in front of your chests while your left fist should be poised close to your left side of your respective chests.

Hold your breath. Move your right fist back close to your left armpit and then flick it forward as though to deliver a back-handed blow to your partner's right cheek bone as you tense your whole body. To prevent the blow from landing on his face your partner uses his right arm to implement a higher than usual blocking action of the Inside Block (*jiap cheen sau tonk*) (*Figure 56*). As your partner blocks your lower right arm you immediately retract your right fist by bending your right arm and bring your right fist close to your left hip. Step forward again with your right foot to your partner's right side. Simultaneously

Figure 56

flex your right arm and make as if sharply to rap the knuckles of your right fist in a back-handed blow against the right side of your partner's ribs (*Figure 57*). Relax and return to your established breathing action.

Figure 57

It is important to note the second step which you should make. This step is a precaution to minimize the risk of counter to your counter even though the attacker would have to be skilled to react in time. The aim is for you to step forward out of harm's way.

After you have gained a working knowledge of the right-handed blow you should try out the technique on the left side. Both you and your partner should take up Dragon Stance with left foot in advance and stand facing one another about twenty-four inches apart.

Position your left fists some twelve inches in front of your chests while the right fists are positioned close to the right side of your respective chests. Hold your breath and tense your body. Move your left fist back near to your right armpit and then flick your fist forward as though to administer a back-handed blow to your partner's left cheekbone with your left fist. Your partner uses his left arm to baulk this blow of yours by utilizing a higher than usual variation of the Inside Block (*jiap cheen sau tonk*).

As soon as your partner effects the blocking action upon your lower left arm with his, directly bend your left arm and move your left fist close to your right hip. Step forward with your left foot to your partner's left side. Concurrently flex your left arm and pretend to strike your partner with the knuckles of your left fist in a back-handed blow aimed at the left side of his ribs. Relax your body and restore your usual breathing rhythm.

After you have gained a thorough knowledge of dealing two successive back-handed blows with the same fist, both by using your left and right fists, you should aim gradually to increase the speed of your actions so that there is hardly a perceptible pause between the two distinct blows. You must exercise the greatest care, when this stage is reached, to see that you do not hurt your partner when trying out the moves at speed.

Unlike the technique immediately preceding this one, the thinking behind this particular combination technique is that your first counter blow is not used in the form of a ruse, but rather as a counter-attack which must be countered in turn by the attacker.

If the attacker does not successfully block, or otherwise avoid your fist, then your object is to hit him. On no account should you train as though your first move will automatically not prove effective. This concept will broaden your general counter-attacking ability so that the attacker would have to defend himself against each and every counter move you made against him – not knowing the imagined from the real danger.

3rd Technique

The response of the attacker to your particular counter move will generally correspond to the degree of stimulus to danger which your counter provokes from his reactions. We know, for instance, that if a feather flutters down towards one's head there is no cause for alarm even if the feather makes contact. This complacent response would certainly not occur if a tile fell off a roof in a gale and descended towards one's head!

In this illustration you lull the attacker into a state of smug complacency by acting as 'the feather', while using a seemingly inept counter move against his face, and then straightaway snap into violent movement by acting as 'the tile' and thus catch him quite unprepared for his true danger.

Both you and your partner stand facing each other some three feet apart with right foot in advance, in the Dragon Stance. Position your right fists about twelve inches in front of your chests with left fists placed just in front of your left hips.

Swing your loosely clenched right fist forward in a slow, clumsy anti-clockwise circular movement so that you miss your partner's chin by the proverbial mile. Continue this inept swinging punch until your right fist nears the front of your left shoulder.

Now you are in earnest, tense your body and hold your breath. Tightly clench your right fist and then flick your lower arm forward in a clockwise back-handed blow so that you could rap the knuckles of your right fist against your partner's right cheekbone (*Figure 58*). Relax and resume breathing.

Perform the compound action of intendedly missing your partner's chin by a wide margin followed quickly by a purposeful backhand blow many times.

After you have used your right fist switch to using your left fist. Stand facing your partner about three feet apart with your left feet in advance in the Dragon Stance. Your left fists should be about twelve inches in front of your chests while your right fists are positioned close to your right hips.

Swing your loosely clenched left fist slowly forward in a clockwise movement and miss your partner's chin by a wide margin. Still the movement of your left fist as it nears your right shoulder. At this juncture hold your breath and

Figure 58

tense your whole body. Tightly clench your left fist then swing it forward in an anti-clockwise movement so that you could deliver a back-handed blow with your left fist being rapped against your partner's left cheekbone.

4th Technique

This particular manoeuvre is most useful to learn since it presupposes that a disadvantageous situation exists for you. It can happen in the hurly burly of an attack that you are caught at some disadvantage, consequently it is sound reasoning and useful in training that you sometimes presume that you cannot always be well balanced or poised to meet an unexpected attack.

In this illustration let us assume that you and your partner are standing facing one another, only about twenty-four inches apart, with right feet in advance in the Dragon Stance. Your right fists are positioned just in front of your chests with left fists close to your left hips.

Request your partner slowly to aim his right fist at your nose. Sway backwards over your left leg and simultaneously bring your bent right arm upwards so that the outside of your right elbow strikes upwards against the inside of your partner's right wrist as your right fist is brought near to your left ear (*Figure 59*). At this stage your bent arm and

Figure 59

right shoulder protect your face, as you take up the Snake Stance with the majority of your weight supported by your bent left leg.

Once you have successfully baulked your partner's right fist with the outside part of your right arm in the way just outlined deal him a quick counter blow with your right fist. Tense your whole body and hold your breath. Flick your right fist forward, in a partial anti-clockwise movement so that you could use a back-handed blow with the knuckles of your right fist striking the right side of your partner's ribs (*Figure 60*). As you make the back-handed blow assume the Dragon Stance.

Figure 60

Immediately after making the blow return your right fist back to a guarding position and relax your body somewhat as you return to the normal breathing action.

Upon completing your initial practice of the technique when using your right arm, switch to using your left arm. Stand facing your partner with left feet forward and about twenty-four inches apart in the Dragon Stance. Your left fists should be somewhat in front of your chests with right fists close to your right hips.

Your partner should slowly move his left fist directly toward your nose. Sway backwards over your right leg as you upraise your bent left arm to knock the outside of your left elbow against the inside of his left wrist. As you baulk his blow in this way, your left fist nears your right ear and your head is almost encompassed within the crook of your left arm and safely protected behind your hunched left shoulder. You adopt the Snake Stance until you make the back-handed blow when you stabilize your posture in the Dragon Stance.

Tense your body and hold your breath. Retaliate by swinging your left fist forward in an anti-clockwise movement so that you could administer a back-handed blow with your left fist against the left side of your partner's ribs. As soon as you have made your counter blow you must return your left fist back to a defensive position.

5th Technique

In this example you are in Dragon Stance when you use a back-handed blow, which is countered, and then quickly follow up with a straight punch.

Both stand facing one another, with your right foot in advance, about three feet apart with right fists just in front of your chests and left fists close to your left hips. Hold your breath then tense your body. Move your right fist to a point near to your left shoulder then flick your fist forward as though to strike your partner's right cheekbone with the knuckles of your right hand in a back-handed blow.

Your partner 'covers up' by shielding his face with his bent right arm and hunches his shoulders. As soon as your partner blocks your right fist, open your hand and grasp his upper sleeve with your right hand. Twist him awkwardly towards his left and your right by pushing your right hand firmly and oppressively against his upper arm. Concurrently with the pushing movement of your right hand punch forward with your left fist aimed at the right side of your partner's back (*Figure 61*). Relax partially and re-introduce your usual breathing action.

Figure 61

After you have become suitably adept at using your right fist to initiate your moves, use your left fist.

Both adopt the Dragon Stance and face one another some three feet apart, with left feet in advance. Your left fists are some twelve inches in front of your chests and right fists positioned close to your right hips. Hold your breath and tense your body. Move your left fist close to your right shoulder before swinging your left fist gently forward in a back-handed blow aimed at your partner's left cheekbone. Your partner blocks your fist by shielding his face with his bent left arm and hunches his shoulders. Immediately that your left fist contacts your partner's left arm, open your hand and tightly clench his left sleeve. Press your left hand oppressively against his upper arm so that he becomes twisted somewhat to his right and your left. At the same time as you use your left hand to grasp his left arm launch a blow with your right fist aimed at the left side of his lower back. Partially relax and revert to normal breathing.

If the attacker is not wearing a coat you would have to grasp his arm close to the elbow joint to momentarily exercise some control over his power of movement.

Once you are able to implement the two separate blows, with barely a noticeable pause, you should try the moves out while moving around your practice area. Remember, however, not to use too forceful actions at an early point in your training.

6th Technique

In this technique a low kicking action is used in conjunction with a high punching movement so that the attacker will have difficulty in preventing your counter-attack.

Stand facing your partner, about two feet apart, with your right foot forward in the Dragon Stance. Adopt a 'southpaw' style with right fist in front of your chest and left fist positioned close to your left hip. Your partner adopts left-foot-forward stance with left fist in front of his chest and right fist positioned close to his right hip.

Tense your body and hold your breath. Make as if slowly to punch your partner on the nose with your right fist. He is meant to deflect your right-handed punch with his left arm in Rising Hand Block (*pah sau tonk*). When your partner prevents your right fist from making contact with his nose you should use the sole of your right foot supposedly to reap his left leg from under him. Go through the motions of this tripping action by swinging your right foot forward in an anti-clockwise movement. Twist your foot so that the little toe of your right foot is nearest the ground, thus enabling you lightly to bring the *sole* of your right foot against the outside of his left ankle (*Figure 62*). The reaping action of your foot, should, in reality, kick the attacker's leg away from under him and cause him to fall to the ground. Relax and resume normal breathing action.

Figure 62

In serious circumstances you must not make the mistake of only going through the motions of making the punching action in the form of a ruse. The first counter-attack must be accomplished by you in a decisive manner in order that you either punch the attacker or he is forced to block or avoid your blow.

After you have become adroit at using your right fist with

which to punch, followed almost simultaneously by your right foot being used in a tripping action, reverse the counter-attacks.

Take up the left-foot-forward stance of the Dragon Stance with left fist in front of your chest and right fist close to your right hip. Your partner ought to assist you by standing facing about twenty-four inches away with his right foot forward in the Dragon Stance. His right fist ought to be in front of his chest with his left fist close to his left hip. Hold your breath and tense your body.

Start your moves by swinging your left foot forward in a clockwise movement so that the sole of your left foot brushes the outside of your partner's right ankle. Remember to twist your left foot so that the little toe of your foot is nearest the ground.

(The presumption is that at this stage, in this variation of the combination technique, you would have caused the attacker to stumble or lose his equilibrium to a greater or lesser degree. Once your forceful tripping action had taken some effect you would immediately be able to make one or more punching actions while the attacker's balance was impaired.)

Move your right fist towards your partner's nose and follow this punch quickly by moving your left fist toward his stomach. After this relax and revert to normal breathing.

You can, as usual, ring the changes so that you accomplish the widely separated and contrary actions with equal facility.

7th Technique

Stand facing your partner with your left leg in advance in the Dragon Stance. Get your partner to stand some four feet away with his right leg forward. Your left fist should be in front of your chest with right fist close to your right hip while your partner's fists are held in the reverse position.

Hold your breath. Be careful not to straighten your body but keep your stance in low profile as you raise your right foot from the ground and advance your right leg so that you achieve a 'snap' stamping action, apparently directed at your partner's right shin and instep. As you perform the stamping action you twist sideways to your partner with your right side nearest to him in Iron Horse Stance and concurrently tense your body so that your whole power is utilized (*Figure 63*). Immediately you have executed the

Figure 63

stamping kick to your partner's right shin, replace your right foot upon the ground so that you adopt the Iron Horse Stance.

Progress by swivelling in an anti-clockwise direction on the ball of your right foot. Keep your left arm reasonably well bent and as your counter-clockwise turn develops rap the back of your left fist against your partner's left cheekbone. At this final stage you will be facing the same direction to which your partner faces. Relax and return to normal breathing.

After you have practised many times using your right foot and left fist to deal your counter blows, reverse your actions in order to practise using your left foot and right fist.

Take up the Dragon Stance with right foot forward. Your right fist is kept in front of your chest while your left fist is in close proximity to your left hip. Get your partner to stand facing you, about four feet away, with his left leg forward.

Hold your breath and tense your body. Advance your left leg, bypassing your right leg and make as though to implement a Stamping Kick with your left foot upon your partner's left shin. You are now positioned sideways to your partner with your left side nearest to him. Make sure that you maintain your low profile stance as you twist counter-clockwise to your right upon the ball of your left foot. When your twisting action develops pretend to rap the back of your right fist against your partner's right cheekbone. Relax and re-institute your normal breathing action.

In training your aim should be to develop a powerful back-handed punch by twisting your body from the hips so that a large portion of your body impetus is embodied in the blow.

8th Technique

Your partner stands facing you, about five feet away with his left leg in advance. You have your left foot forward in the Dragon Stance. Your partner should step forward upon his right leg bypassing his left foot and make as if to administer a punch to your chest with his right fist.

As your partner punches forward with his right fist you withdraw your left leg outwards and diagonally backwards to the direction of his advance and adopt the Iron Horse Stance. Hold your breath and tense your body. Open your right hand and keep the palm facing forward as you rotate your lower right arm in a clockwise movement so that the little-finger edge of your right hand contacts the outside part of his right wrist (*Figure 64*). After you have effected this blocking action with the edge of your right hand, grip his lower right sleeve (or wrist) with your right hand and maintain this grip until the completion of your counter moves. This precaution is to prevent him using a back-handed blow with his right fist to your face.

Figure 64

Continue your counter moves by raising your right foot from the ground before you make as if to deliver a side kick with the sole of your right foot to the right side of your partner's ribs (*Figure 65*). Speedily replace your right foot back on the ground and then make a 'snap' punch with your left fist directed at his ribs while you concurrently twist your hips to the right for additional power. Make certain that you retract your left fist immediately after the punching action has seemingly been effected to his ribs. Relax and breathe normally once again.

Complete your moves by releasing your partner's right sleeve (or wrist) from the grasp of your right hand and back away from him into the left-foot-forward stance with left fist forward.

Figure 65

Now prepare to substitute left for right where necessary. Face one another, about five feet apart, both with your right legs in advance in the Dragon Stance. Request your partner to step a large pace forward with his left leg, by-passing his right leg before making a punch toward your chest with his left fist. When your partner's left fist nears your chest you should move your right leg outwards and diagonally backwards to the direction of his advance as you assume the Iron Horse Stance. Hold your breath and tense your body. Open your left hand and rotate your lower left arm in an anti-clockwise action in order that the little-finger edge of your left hand contacts the outside of his left wrist. As the action of your left hand brushes his left fist away from your chest grasp his lower left sleeve, or wrist, with your left hand and retain this restriction upon his left arm throughout the remainder of your counter technique.

Raise your left foot from the ground and go through the motions of making a side kick with the sole of your left foot directed at your partner's ribs. As soon as you have performed the kicking action with your left foot quickly replace your foot back upon the ground. Once you have resumed your strongly balanced stance make a 'snap' punch with your right fist to his ribs. Relax and revert to your normal breathing action.

Finalize your moves by releasing your partner's left sleeve or wrist and back away from your partner into right-foot-forward stance of the Dragon Stance.

9th Technique

This is a further example in the tactic of continuing to counter the attacker even when you have been placed at some disadvantage. In this illustration you are presupposed to have become twisted partially sideways to the attacker, after having managed to prevent him from unexpectedly kicking you in the stomach.

Stand facing each other, about four feet apart, with left feet in advance in the Dragon Stance. Ask your partner slowly to move his right foot forward as though to kick you in the middle of your stomach. Move your left foot a small pace directly outwards to your left and twist round on the balls of your feet rather too much to your right. Hold your breath and tense your body. Open your left hand and use the little-finger edge of your hand to thrust against your partner's right calf so that you prevent his right foot from contacting with your stomach. At this stage you will be at right angles to your partner with your left side nearest to him (*Figure 66*).

Figure 66

Make progress by continuing to pivot forward to your right upon the soles of your feet and step backwards with your right foot as you come almost to complete a circular turn. Move your clenched right fist toward your left hip prior to swinging the fist forward, as though to use a back-handed blow to rap the knuckles of your right fist against your partner's right cheekbone (*Figure 67*).

Straightaway after making the blow step diagonally forward with your left leg, to the direction behind your partner's back, and immediately take up a guarding position for any possible retaliatory blows. Continue to move away from him to a distance of say two yards. Relax and resume normal breathing.

After you have become proficient at using your right fist to regain the initiative and at moving smoothly out of harm's way, perform the counter by using your left fist.

Figure 67

Stand facing one another at a suitable distance both with your right foot in advance in the Dragon Stance. Ask your partner to make as if to kick you in the stomach with his left foot. Step a small pace outwards with your right foot before twisting a little too far to your left. Hold your breath and tense your body. Open your right hand before swinging the little-finger edge of the hand into contact with his left calf so that his foot passes harmlessly in front of your stomach.

Upon completion of this movement you will be twisted sideways to your partner with your right side nearest him.

Continue to pivot around to your left upon the soles of your feet and then step backwards with your left leg as you practically make a complete counter-clockwise turning action. Move your left fist to your right hip then swing your left fist forward as though to deliver a back-handed blow with your left fist against your partner's left cheek-bone. Instantly after making this blow with your left fist, step diagonally forward with your right leg to the direction behind your partner's back and take care to adopt a self-protective posture as you continue to move away from your partner. Relax and breathe normally.

10th Technique

Let us assume again, that after diverting a totally unexpected blow, this time a punch, you become twisted sideways too much.

Stand facing your partner, about twenty-four inches apart with your left foot in advance in Dragon Stance while he has his right foot in advance. Ask your partner to make a punch with his right fist directly towards your stomach. Tense your body and hold your breath. Prevent his fist from contact with your stomach by swinging your lower left arm inwards, so that your lower arm is vertical to the ground, with fist twisted downward in the Inside Block (*jiap cheen sau tonk*). The little-finger edge of your left wrist contacts the same part of his right wrist (*Figure 68*). When your warding-off action takes effect, twist overmuch to your right both to add power to your actions and also as though you have made a small, but critical, error in positioning. Do not try to adjust your position by squarely facing your partner but instead continue to twist to your right and move your right foot backwards as you twist through about 270° – say three quarters of one complete circle. As your clockwise turning action develops, poke your right elbow into the right side of your partner's ribs

Figure 68

in a backward blow (*Figure 69*). Relax and resume normal breathing.

You should try out the blocking action and the counter blow many times in order to familiarize yourself with the moves.

Once you have become adept at utilizing the left arm block and counter blow with your right elbow, alternate by using your right arm and left elbow.

Stand opposite your partner with your right foot forward while he stands about two feet away in the Dragon Stance with his left foot forward. Request your partner to punch forward with his left fist precisely at your breastbone. Tense your body as you hold your breath. Baulk his blow by twisting your lower right arm inwards in Inside Block (*jiap cheen sau tonk*) so that your lower arm is vertical to the

Figure 69

ground with fist nearest the surface. By this purposeful twisting action of your arm the little-finger edge of your right wrist contacts the same part of his wrist. At this point the supposition is that while you have successfully parried your partner's punch, you have twisted sideways too much with your right side nearest to him.

Continue to twist about to your left and move your left foot backwards as you almost complete your about turn through three quarters of one complete circle. Once your counter-clockwise turning action has developed sufficiently, move your left elbow backwards to poke the left side of your partner's ribs. Relax and reproduce your normal breathing action.

The complete activity consists of making your retaliatory

elbow with barely a perceptible pause in your actions after you have prevented the punch from being landed.

11th Technique

The attacker is presumed to lash out with a foot against your stomach, in this instance, which you counter in your turn by using Downward Cross Armed Block (*sub jee sau luk tonk*). You then use your knee to administer a counter-attack.

It is, perhaps, significant here to note that an acquaintance of mine has a natural aptitude for implementing this blocking action in a tremendously effective manner. In essence he hunches his shoulders, to generate enormous power, before he punches downward with his fists while suddenly dropping his shoulders and tensing his whole body. I saw him demonstrate his excellent technique many times against a recognized young champion, who was thus prevented from scoring with a kicking action against him.

Stand facing your partner with left foot forward in the Dragon Stance while he stands about three feet away with his left foot forward. He should initiate the action by moving his right foot forward as if to kick you in the stomach. Cross your arms at the wrists, so that your right wrist is uppermost, then move your clenched fists close to the front of your right shoulder. Your right fist ought to be pressed closely to your right shoulder as you hunch your shoulders and prepare to make the blocking action.

Hold your breath. Move your crossed lower arms diagonally downwards by punching downwards with your fists as you 'drop' your shoulders, and exhale while tensing your whole body. Ascertain that only light contact is made with the front of your partner's right shin with the little finger edge of your right wrist (*Figure 70*).

Immediately after you have made the blocking action, move your clenched fists, with arms still crossed at wrists, towards your partner's throat so that the little-finger edge of your right wrist gently comes to rest against the front of his throat. Unclench your hands and grip his jacket at the shoulder, still keeping your arms crossed at the wrists. Maintain your balance firmly upon your slightly bent left leg as you make the pretence of bringing your right knee upwards and forward into your partner's stomach while pulling him into the blow with your hands.

Figure 70

Disengage after you have made as if to bring your knee into your partner and relax partially as you return to normal breathing.

Now try out the technique when your partner tries to kick you with his left foot in the stomach.

Take up the Dragon Stance with your right foot advanced, opposite your partner, who is standing about three feet away with his right foot forward. He makes his attack by attempting to move his left foot slowly toward your stomach.

Cross your arms at the wrists, in the same way as before, but this time move your clenched fists close to the front of your left shoulder as you hunch your shoulders. Hold your breath. Punch with your fists diagonally downwards, while you 'drop' your shoulders, and again remember to exhale and tense your body just before you make slight contact with your partner's left shin with the little-finger edge of your right wrist.

As soon as you have achieved light contact with your partner's left shin, move your clenched fists toward your partner's throat so that the little-finger edge of your right wrist again rests against your partner's throat. Still keep your arms crossed at the wrists, as you unclench your hands, before grasping his jacket at the shoulder. Stabilize your balance by firmly supporting the weight of your body on your slightly bent right leg before launching your left knee forward and upward toward your partner's stomach as you tug at his jacket with your hands to achieve a contrary action for added power. Immediately after you have made the apparent counter stroke, disengage your hold on your partner, relax somewhat and breathe normally again.

It is worth noting that if the attacker is not wearing clothing on his upper body, one only need cup the hands around the top of his shoulders in order to add to the power of your counter blow by exerting a contrary force against his body.

12th Technique

Let us suppose that the attacker lunges forward and attempts to kick you in the region of your stomach. Your riposte is to divert his foot past your front or side, as you glide forward partially inside his leg and flick your fist into his groin followed by a punch to his face.

With the forward momentum generated by the attacker, when he makes a totally committed lunging kick, it is generally a sound tactic to divert rather than attempt to baulk the attacker's oncoming foot.

Stand facing your partner with left foot forward in the

Dragon Stance while he stands about a yard away with his left leg in advance.

Your partner should slowly lunge forward, as though to kick you in the area of your stomach with his right foot, while totally committing his balance forward with his right leg kept extended. Hold your breath and tense your body. Start your counter by unclenching your right hand and use the flat of your hand to sweep his right leg to your left by connecting with the inside part of his right calf in Palm Block (*han sau pun tonk*) (*Figure 71*). As his right foot is deflected away from your stomach and your partner allows his right foot to return to the ground, twist somewhat to your right and glide your right foot forward so that you get inside his lower leg. Make your right hand into

Figure 71

a fist again and flick the back of your fist against his groin or stomach.

After you have made the back-handed blow retract your right fist to your right hip. Twist to your right and stabilize your balance as you make a 'snap' punch with your left fist directed toward your partner's nose. Relax and revert to normal breathing as you back away out of range of your partner's feet.

Now get ready to try out the counter when your partner kicks toward your stomach with his left foot. Take up the Dragon Stance with your right foot forward while your partner stands about a yard away with his right leg forward. He should extend his left leg and make the preliminary attack by slowly lunging forward with the supposed intention of kicking you in the stomach. Hold your breath and tense your body. Open your left hand, keeping your fingers pressed together and sweep the flat of your hand against the inside of his left calf with Palm Block (*han sau pun tonk*) so that his left foot and lower leg are knocked outwards. Glide forward on your left foot and then clench the fingers of your left hand to form a fist as you twist partially toward your partner. Flick the back of your left fist into his groin or stomach. After making the presumed blow, instantly retract your left fist to your left hip. Twist slightly to your left and stabilize your balance prior to making a punching action with your right fist aimed precisely at your partner's nose. Relax and resume normal breathing as you back away out of range of your partner's feet.

13th Technique

Let us visualize that the attacker has managed to get close enough for him to grip your lapels preparatory to butting you in the face with his head.

It is absolutely vital that you do not permit the attacker to butt you in the face, as more often than not you would become incapacitated to a marked degree. You can generally assume that anyone who makes as if to grip your lapels intends to butt you in the face. Naturally, if you know a man to be notorious for butting people you must keep him from getting too close by effectively using your feet or hands. Do not ever hesitate for an instant to give such an attacker the benefit of the doubt if he manages to get to close quarters, but deal with him immediately by the following method of defence.

Ask your partner to stand facing you about twelve inches away and then to grasp your opposing lapels with his hands, as he hunches his shoulders, bends his legs and keeps his arms well bent. These movements will place him in the strongest possible position, but this adverse situation is requisite if you are to achieve absolute realism in training to meet with such an attack.

Tense your whole body and hold your breath. You must interpose your right arm between your partner's head and your face. Achieve this by literally punching diagonally forward with your right fist over your partner's right shoulder as you twist slightly to your left and bend your legs. While you must be careful to see that your elbow does not connect forcibly with your partner's face, no such consideration should be allowed the attacker. If your arm is kept slightly bent and very rigid you will be able to deliver a jarring blow with your elbow or forearm to the attacker's face or head. In addition, by the very rigidity of your right arm you will prevent his head from being moved forward as you tense your whole body when your forceful arm movement is implemented (*Figure 72*).

Even after you have delivered such a blow as the one just described, you must continue to deal with the attacker to ensure he is rendered incapable of hurting you.

After the outside portion of your arm connects with his face, prepare to trip him to the ground. A few words of caution are appropriate at this point. Do not try to implement this second counter too soon against the attacker, by skimping over the essential arm action just described, as this would prove dangerous to you. There is relatively plenty of time after your arm blow has been used, to follow with the counter move now to be described.

You are presumed to be in close contact with your

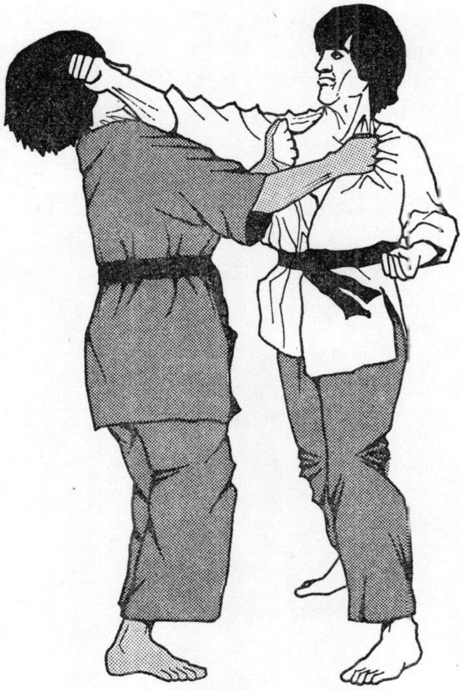

Figure 72

partner after supposedly using your arm to prevent his butting you in the face. Place all of your body weight on your left leg and swing the sole of your right foot, in a reasonably large movement, as though to reap powerfully forward against either the front or side of his left ankle. When the reaping action of your right foot is made, gently use the outside of your right arm to knock or push your partner's head and upper body to the contrary direction to which his legs are becoming moved to (*Figure 73*).

Do not be unduly concerned about the fact that an attacker may still be holding your lapels. The fear of falling would generally impel him to let go of your lapels, so that he could then use his arms to protect himself from the fall. If he does not relinquish his grip on your clothing simply keep very close to him and fall on him.

In my experience it is not necessary to bother too much as to where precisely your right foot strikes the attacker's leg or legs, provided a large, forceful and unexpected movement is used. If you happen to be in bare feet, or wearing

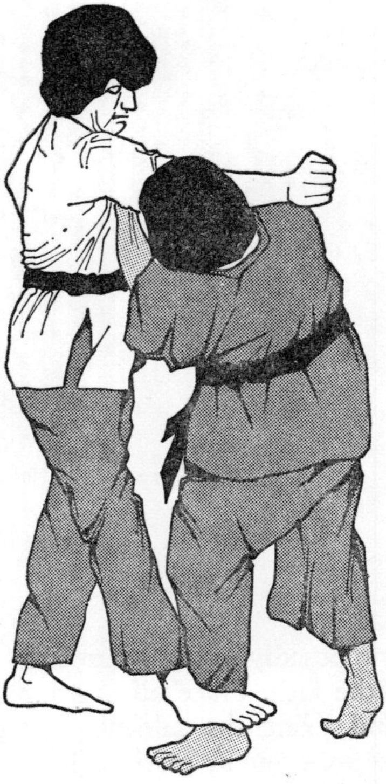

Figure 73

soft footwear, the sole of your foot is best used; whereas, if you are wearing shoes, then the inside edge of your hard footwear can be used in a scythe-like action with a very telling effect. Should it prove necessary, a couple of kicking actions could be implemented in order to knock the attacker to the ground.

14th Technique

For explanatory purposes let's take it that you are faced by the attacker armed with a knife or sharp pointed weapon.

There is a general fallacy, possibly created by the media, that the attacker armed with a knife invariably upraises his arm before striking downwards with the weapon aimed at the defender's chest. While this large movement looks both visually spectacular and lends itself to counter, by the Palm Block followed by a kick, it is largely fictional. In cold reality the usual and very dangerous form of attack is that the knife is thrust at the defender's stomach in a horizontal (or even more dangerously upwards) movement.

Here are some hints for putting such a man, who uses this form of knife attack, momentarily to disadvantage.

If you are close to a chair or other portable piece of furniture you can, of course, use this sort of object to defend yourself or others with. Should you have loose change in your pocket you can use this to hurl at the attacker's face to distract him as you make a counter kick against him. Even the innocuous glass of water is useful as a diversionary tactic. Out of doors, loose earth or sand used in the same way would also provide a momentarily, and perhaps crucial, pause for you to counter-attack. A brief-case, book or similar object can also be used to thwart the attack, by being thrown at the attacker's face. An umbrella can be flicked open and thrust at the attacker with the ferrule end toward him as you follow up behind the screen so provided with powerful low-level kicking actions. An outer garment, being carried on the arm, can either be used by spreading it out as you drape it over the attacker's head, or, alternatively you can wind it around your lower left arm which you then use to stave off the most dangerous thrusts made by the attacker.

In the unlikely event that the attacker faces you while holding the knife in his upraised right hand, with thumb uppermost, you can presume with relative safety that he intends either a downward blow to your chest, or a backward clockwise blow emanating from the left side of his body toward your right side or stomach.

The downward blow is best nullified by using the previously described Back Palm Block (*sau pun hau tonk*) followed by either front or side kick. The backward blow is best countered by jumping back out of harm's way and immediately delivering a kicking action to the middle of the attacker's body as his arm action still continues. Continuously try out the foregoing two moves, with your partner holding a harmless make-believe 'knife' and get used to the actions called for.

Now let us give our attention to the much more likely attack of the knife being thrust unexpectedly at your stomach, when you are compelled entirely by circumstances to rely on your own capabilities. There are two blocking actions which I consider relatively safe to use against a knife thrust aimed at the stomach. These are Palm Block (*han sau pun tonk*) and Downward Block (*ti sau tonk*). I suggest that you get your partner to hold the so-called knife in his right hand and try out both of these blocking actions to see which one suits your own physical capabilities and then thoroughly to practise the defensive movement of your choice. The illustration depicts Palm Block (*han sau pun tonk*) (*Figure 74*).

Remember that in the case of this attack it is a cardinal error not to move your body to one side when you use a blocking action, lest your arm misses the attacker's arm and the weapon pierces or cuts your body. Consequently you must practise springing to one side as you implement the blocking movement which you have selected.

Once you have countered the thrust of a knife you must deliver one or more kicks to the middle of the attacker's body to incapacitate him temporarily in order to preclude him from any further attack.

15th Technique

This particular illustration is really a compound defensive technique dealing with the contingency that arises when the attacker grasps a part of your body or clothing with one or both hands, from front, side or rear.

Here are some tactics for you to consider and practise with your partner.

Figure 74

If one of your arms is held by a recognizably strong attacker, do not attempt to free yourself from the encumbrance of his hold. Instead use an elbow blow delivered to his face or body by your free arm or use your knee or foot to administer a blow. The choice of blow is dependent upon the distance separating you.

When the attacker holds both of your arms lash out with your feet or bring your knee upwards if he is close and in front of you.

Should the attacker be behind you and wrap his arms around you from behind, either over or under your arms, use Stamping Kick. Do this by raising a foot from the ground then turn it outwards prior to scraping the outside edge of your foot downwards into his shin. Finalize your movement by grinding your heel into his corresponding instep (*Figure 75*). Backward elbow blows delivered to the attacker's face finalize this counter.

Figure 75

Once the attacker grabs your hair from behind, your first action must be to press the wrist and hand which he is using close to your head, to stop him wrenching your hair and disturbing your balance to your rear. Bend your legs as you run diagonally backwards past either of his sides, and deliver a well placed kick as you awkwardly twist his wrist (*Figure 76*).

16th Technique

Up to now in this book, I have purposely placed the principal emphasis on a defensive strategy which has involved

Figure 76

your using a blocking action against the original blow made by the attacker. While this type of defence forms an integral and vital part of Kung Fu training, there is the equally effective technique of avoiding the attacker's blows before quickly retaliating.

This technique 'in getting out of harm's way' is not easy for the beginner to acquire until he has gained a sound training in the basic blocking actions because of the degree of co-ordination required. Once you become well versed in the art you will tend more and more to avoid blows rather than block them.

While the two basic concepts of either blocking or avoiding an attack are entirely separate methods, more often than not the system of avoiding as a defensive tactic can be merged with blocking actions so that one uses technique from both styles. When you try to avoid a particular attack you can thus still be prepared to use a blocking movement if you do not manage to elude the attack. On the other side of the coin, as it were, a blocking action is generally a total commitment and does not consequently lend itself for you quickly to change it into an avoiding tactic.

Masters with many years training behind them generally avoid attacks with a side step or by swaying the body out of harm's way. Just for one of the few exceptions, the performance of the following technique requires you to move directly backwards.

Let us consider the concept of avoiding, as opposed to blocking, an attack when the attacker makes Front Kick (*cheen keck tek*) against the middle of your body and you respond with the same technique against him.

Stand facing your partner about two yards away from him with your left foot in advance in the Dragon Stance. Position your unclenched left hand about twelve inches in front of your chest and unclenched right hand by your right hip. Your partner should stand facing you with his right foot forward.

Ask your partner to step forward, with exaggerated slowness, onto his left foot and then with equal slowness to kick with his right foot directly at your stomach. As your partner makes his initial step with his left foot and prepares slowly to kick you with his right foot you must move your left foot a small pace quickly backwards followed by your right foot being taken backwards past the inside of your left foot. As your evading action causes your partner's right foot not to reach your stomach, he should allow his foot to drop down onto the ground well in front of his left foot. Hold your breath and tense your body.

You now quickly retaliate by hopping a small pace forward on your left foot and make as if to kick your partner in the stomach with your right foot. Relax and resume normal breathing.

After you have made your counter kicking-action, back away from your partner to a distance of about two yards.

Your right unclenched hand should be positioned about twelve inches in front of your chest with your opened left hand close to your left hip. Take up the Dragon Stance with your right foot forward while your partner assumes the Dragon Stance with his left foot in advance.

Your partner ought to step forward onto his right foot before slowly aiming his left foot toward your stomach. When your partner steps toward you with his right foot, you must retract your right foot quickly and immediately follow this by also moving your left foot backwards to bypass the inside of your right foot. After your avoiding action causes your partner's left foot to fall short of your stomach, as it were, your partner should allow his foot to return to the floor. Hold your breath and tense your body. Now speedily respond with a counter kick. Hop forward a small pace with your right foot before launching your left foot towards your partner's stomach. Immediately after making your kicking action move away from your partner. Relax and return to normal breathing action.

Your partner can prove of great help to you if he endeavours to synchronize his actions with yours. Once you achieve a rhythmic movement in avoiding the kicking actions, before responding in kind, you will gradually become automatically used to carrying out the necessary actions. On no account should you try to catch one another unawares at this stage in training. It is vital to help one another in the initial stages of training so that you both become acclimatized to implementing the kicking actions. The essential point constantly to bear in mind is that seeming retaliation by you is immediate after first having avoided your partner's kicking actions.

After some time spent in training you will find it practicable to remain quite unflurried even when your partner speeds up his actions and tries properly to kick you in the stomach.

17th Technique

Here is another avoiding tactic for use when the attacker tries to kick you in the stomach. On this occasion, however, you use a side stepping technique rather than moving backwards. Ask your partner to stand facing you at about two yards distance with his right foot forward in the Dragon Stance. You take up the Dragon Stance with your left foot forward while positioning your unclenched left hand about ten inches in front of the left side of your chest and unclenched right hand by your right hip.

You should aim to avoid your partner's right foot by assuming the Snake Stance, with about 70 per cent of your weight borne by your right leg and 30 per cent on your forward leg, while twisting a quarter turn to your right to face the direction beyond your partner's left side.

Your partner should now step forward upon his left foot before slowly moving his right foot directly toward the centre of your stomach. As he makes the kicking motion you must avoid his oncoming foot. Achieve your avoiding action by spinning inwards to your right on the ball of your left foot as you withdraw your right leg backwards in a clockwise direction so that you face to the right of the original direction to which you were facing. At this stage you must support the majority of your weight on your bent right leg. The transfer of the major portion of your weight to your right leg, coupled with a slightly rearward inclination of your body, will also tend to move your body away from the kick. The palm of your left hand can also be brought into a defensive position for extra safety (*Figure 77*).

Once you have successfully caused your partner's right foot to pass harmlessly in front of your stomach you are in a position to institute your counter. Your partner allows his right foot to drop to the ground when he does not achieve contact. In this example you should use a variation of Front Kick (*cheek keck tek*).

Hold your breath and tense your body. Stabilize your posture by supporting your body weight upon your bent right leg, then upraise your bent left leg until your left knee is level with your hips. Then flex your leg as you flick the toes of your left foot forward at your partner's side, back or stomach. Relax and re-start your normal breathing action.

You immediately back-off when you make your counter strike and prepare once again to avoid his right foot. After many repetitions of evading your partner's right foot, switch your actions so that you get used to the necessary moves for avoiding a kick from his left foot.

Figure 77

Stand facing your partner, about two yards away from him with your right foot forward while your partner has his left foot forward. Both of you adopt Dragon Stance while you, for your part, should also position your unclenched hands so that your right hand is some twelve inches in front of your chest with left hand by your left hip.

Your partner initiates his kicking action by stepping forward with his right foot before slowly aiming the toes of his left foot directly towards your stomach. You cause his kick to miss by carrying out the following moves.

Pivot inwards, to your left, on the ball of your right foot while withdrawing your left leg backwards in a counter-clockwise direction until you face to the left of the original direction to which you were facing. Your left leg now supports the major portion of your body weight and you have taken up the Snake Stance.

Once you have successfully caused your partner's left foot to miss your stomach, your partner allows his foot gently to drop back to the ground.

Hold your breath and tense your body. You finalize your counter by delivering the variant of Front Kick (*cheen keck tek*) to your partner's body with your right foot. Remember that your knee is raised before you flick the lower leg forward supposedly to deliver a kick with the front part of your right foot.

I urge you to spare no effort in gaining mastery in this technique and the one immediately preceding, since their use in your defensive strategy will negate what often prove to be very dangerous forms of attack. Moreover, a supplementary benefit which you will find to be gradually derived by constant practice, is that you will develop the attribute of swaying and moving away from various forms of blows which in the beginning would have reached your body with painful results.

18th Technique

The attacker grasps your jacket lapel with one hand while preparing to punch you in the face with his other hand. The aims of such an attacker are to boost his own confidence while trying to overawe you by gripping your jacket lapel. A further aim is to use a contrary movement by tugging you forward into his punch.

You counter this form of attack by using a throwing action to the attacker's rear in order to take advantage of his pulling action upon your coat.

Stand facing your partner at close quarters and ask him to grasp your right lapel with his left hand and make as if to punch you in the face with his right fist. Your first priority is to block your partner's right arm so that he could not hit you in the face even if he so intended. When your partner moves his right fist slowly toward your face, open your left hand and bring the little-finger edge of your left hand against the hollow formed by his right elbow so that his right arm is momentarily stopped from moving forward.

Immediately after you have stilled the movement of his arm with your left hand in the way just described, grip his right sleeve or elbow joint.

Grasp your partner's left lapel with your right hand then concurrently step smoothly forward with your left foot to place it on the ground only six inches away from the outside of your partner's right foot. Supporting the whole weight of your body upon your slightly bent left leg, swing your straightened right leg forward between your own left leg and your partner's right leg. The action of your right leg should be like a pendulum, so that you swing it forward and then quickly backward so that the back of your right thigh can be dashed against the back of your partner's thigh. Simultaneously with the reaping action of your right leg you tilt your partner's upper body over to his right with your hands so that you could throw him backwards to the ground as you tense your whole body (*Figure 78*).

You should become suitably fast in the execution of this counter by constantly blocking, gripping and implementing the throwing movement in one smooth and continuous compound action when your partner grips your right lapel with his left hand.

Now try the moves when your partner grabs your left lapel with his right hand while preparing to hit you in the face with his left fist. On this occasion, for this particular attack, I do not consider it necessary to implement your counter move against your partner's other side. All that you need do is to block his left-handed punch with your right hand cut into his left elbow joint. You then grip both of his sleeves with your hands, as you step forward to his right side with your left foot, before apparently tripping him backwards over your right thigh, which is

Figure 78

dashed into contact with the back of his right thigh. Naturally, you must take care not to hurl your partner backwards to the ground when trying out this technique.

19th Technique

Sometimes a drunk, possibly aggressive, bully attempts to overawe an innocent passerby, by leaning over him while clasping his hands oppressively downward upon the other's shoulders or chest. Here is a not too drastic a counter for you to effect an escape from such an inebriated customer's clutches!

Ask your partner to stand facing you about two feet

away and then to make as if to rest his hands on your shoulders. Grasp the inside of his sleeves close to his elbow joints with your hands before stepping a fairly large pace outwards with your right foot while twisting the foot inwards so that it almost points directly to your left. Support the whole weight of your body on your slightly bent right leg as you twist your left foot so that the little toe is nearest the ground, and bring the sole of your left foot against the front of his right ankle. Stretch your body somewhat so that you could trip your partner over your outstretched left foot by tugging sharply at his sleeves in the general direction toward your left ear (*Figure 79*).

After you have assiduously practised the tripping action by using your left leg, switch to using your right leg. Again

Figure 79

grab your partner's sleeves as he attempts to lay his hands upon you. Step outwards to your left with your left foot as you turn the foot inwards and transfer the whole of your weight to your partially bent left leg. Move the sole of your right foot, with little toe nearest the ground, into light contact with the front of your partner's left ankle. Tug at your partner's sleeves so that you could trip him over your outstretched right foot to the ground.

While the counter throwing action just outlined appears to be quite innocuous on summary consideration, it can be very usefully utilized on numerous occasions at the very outset of attacking movements made against you. No contact is made with the attacker other than through the medium of the hands and a foot and this does lend itself to quickness in application. The essential points to bear in mind are that you use maximum leverage and move out of the way as your contrary pressure begins to take effect upon the attacker.

20th Technique

Let us picture that the attacker grasps your throat with both hands from the front and tries to throttle you by pressing his thumbs against your windpipe.

In this event it is important to note that the grip is generally strongest when the attacker is permitted to keep his arms bent, in which circumstance he can exert his strength against your neck. Instead of moving away, which is not always practicable, the first basic counter-attack now outlined is calculated to bend the attacker's arms even more than he intended.

Ask your partner to stand facing you at close range and then tightly to grasp the front of your throat with both of his hands.

Maintain a strongly balanced stance as you clench your hands tightly to form them into compact fists. Raise your fists in front of you above your partner's arms with knuckles twisted inward so that the little-finger edges of your wrists are nearest to the ground.

Now make as if to use a double fisted 'hammer blow' by bringing your clenched fists downward upon your partner's forearms. When you go through the motions of making these blows, even though you do not use force, you should still raise your shoulders before slumping them downwards as you tense your whole body just as the blows are struck (*Figure 80*). As your partner leans forward, through the gentle impact of your blows upon his arms you *carefully* go through the action of flicking the backs of your fists into his face. Do this by pressing the knuckles of your fists together before moving your fists upward and outward.

Figure 80

In actuality the forceful implementation of your hammer blows would disrupt the attacker's hold about your neck by knocking his hands downwards and also force his upper body to become inclined even more forward.

When your backhanded blows seemingly cause your partner to recoil you are able to use Front Kick (*cheen keck tek*) finally to complete your counter-attack.

If you are opposed by a much stronger adversary it is noteworthy that you can literally beat upon his arms with your fists as you intersperse these actions with backhanded blows to his face. In addition a foot or knee can also be brought into play in order quickly to disrupt the dangerous chokehold.

In the following alternative defensive method, the presumed attacker may be very much taller than you or, alternatively, he may be slow moving or otherwise inept, which enables you to manage to bring the following counter move into action while he is either actually reaching for you or has not quite managed to get a firm grip upon your throat. If the attacker is tall or inept you can successfully use a variant of Rising Hand Block (*pah sau tonk*) followed with Hammer Blows and Double Handed Punch.

Ask your partner to stand about twenty-four inches away from you prior to reaching forward with his hands to grasp your throat.

Bend your legs well to create a strong posture then bring your tightly clenched fists forward in front of your chest in such a way that the thumbs are uppermost and the fists are close together. With hardly a pause, upraise your bent arms as you twist your fists inwards so that the thumbs become turned nearest to the ground as the outside of your wrists come into contact with the inside portion of your partner's lower arms. Once these combined blocking actions of Rising Hand Block (*pah sau tonk*) take effect and compel your partner's hands and lower arms to be jogged upwards away from your neck, you are ready to implement your counter blows.

Quickly move your clenched fists outwards and slightly downwards so that your hands are held widely apart with fists twisted so that the palms of your hands are facing outwards. Speedily move your fists downward and inward while twisting them so that your palms become uppermost and the little finger edge of your fists could strike against each side of your partner's ribs in the Hammer Blow.

As soon as you have made as if to strike your partner in each side of his ribs, you withdraw your fists, still palms uppermost, to their respective hips. You finalize your moves by twisting your fists so that knuckles become uppermost as you punch directly forward at the middle of your partner's body with both of your clenched fists.

21st Technique

When a strong attacker applies this widely known headlock with one arm, while pummelling the defender's face with the fist of his unencumbered arm, it can prove to be a deadly form of attack to which the defender could quite easily succumb.

The essential point constantly to bear in mind with regard to nullifying this form of attack is that the actual hold, although irksome, must be ignored until the attacker has been prevented from hitting your face with his fist.

Ask your partner to stand close to your right side while facing the same direction which you face. He should wrap his left arm tightly around your neck before pulling your head downward to his left hip where he encompasses your head within the crook of his left arm. Your partner should maintain his firm hold upon your neck, which in turn restricts you from moving your head, before he makes as if continuously to punch you in the face with his right fist. Your first priority is to prevent your partner from punching you in the face with his right fist by tightly clutching his right sleeve with your left hand. The importance of holding a sleeve, in preference to the arm, should be noted. It is much easier to restrict punches if clothing is tightly clasped against the arm being used to punch with. If no clothing is worn by the attacker, it is best to grasp the elbow joint.

Continue your counter moves by moving your unclenched right hand upwards behind your partner's back and then over his left shoulder. Lodge the little-finger edge of your right hand under your partner'snose then use oppressive applied pressure at an angle of between 30°–45° in relation to the ground, to force his head backwards so that he becomes awkwardly bent over backwards.

Twist your right knee outwards and jog it against the back of your partner's left knee so as to disrupt his balance so that he becomes stretched over backwards, like a string in a bow, across your out-turned bent right leg (*Figure 81*).

Figure 81

Continue your counter stroke by upraising your clenched left fist then bring it speedily downwards as though to deliver a Hammer Blow with the little-finger edge of your left fist contacting his unguarded stomach. Finalize your actions by thrusting your lower left arm against your partner's chest as you use the sole of your right foot gently to reap either or both of his legs from under him.

After you have tried out the defence when your partner grabs your head from your right side, as just outlined, ask him to stand by your left shoulder.

Your partner should tightly encompass your neck within his bent right arm as he pulls your head down to his right hip and makes as if to punch you in the face with his left fist. Grasp his left sleeve securely with your right hand to foil his aim of striking you with his left fist.

Move your unclenched left hand upwards behind your partner's back and then over his right shoulder. Lodge the little finger of your left hand under your partner's nose. Move the edge of your left hand upwards against your partner's nose as you twist your left knee outwards before jogging your left knee against the back of your partner's right knee. Once you have stretched your partner's body awkwardly backwards upraise your clenched right fist before moving it quickly downward as though to strike your partner's exposed stomach with the little-finger edge of your fist in a 'Hammer Blow'.

Finalize your actions by using your left forearm to press against your partner's chest and use the sole of your left foot gently to reap one or both of his legs from under him.

If the wily attacker twists his head sideways to prevent you from lodging your hand under his nose you can still effect your escape from the hold by pressing the tips of your fingers against his nearest eye. In a dangerous predicament, not of your own making, the natural amount of distaste you may feel even in applying light pressure to the attacker's eye must be overcome. If one is concerned too much over the nicety of pressing the attacker's eye, without causing damage, to bend him backwards, it is quite feasible that escape from this rather dangerous hold would prove impossible in time to avoid suffering serious injury.

22nd Technique

Should you be knocked or thrown to the ground during the course of an attack, it can prove to be very dangerous for you. It is of paramount importance that if you fall to the ground, the standing attacker is not permitted to kick you in the head or body before you have the opportunity to regain your feet.

Ask your partner, very gently and with controlled slowness, to trip you to the ground. As soon as your back contacts the surface swivel round so that your feet are brought nearest to your partner. Twist over somewhat on your left side keeping your legs only slightly bent, with left foot about six inches from the surface, and right foot about eighteen inches from the ground.

Your partner can help you to gain an all-round defensive ability if he now slowly moves round you in a clockwise circular movement. As he moves around swivel on your buttocks and use your lower arms to follow him so that your feet are kept nearest him. It is not efficient if you try to keep your feet constantly in the recommended position as you move around, rather it is best sometimes to alternate this with using a sudden scissor-like motion of your legs to 'catch up' with your partner. Occasionally you should place a foot upon the ground in order to gain purchase from the surface to aid your efforts to propel yourself around in a complete circle.

After several separate and full circular revolutions you should request your partner slowly to reverse his direction of rotation by moving in an anti-clockwise circular action while you scrupulously keep your feet nearest to him. On no account ought you to keep the whole of your back on the ground as you swivel around, as otherwise your power of movement becomes impeded. You should alternate with your right foot higher than your left foot in relation to the ground while now and then switching to keep your left foot higher than your right foot.

If you have sometimes to flip your legs over your head by accomplishing a 'backward roll', quickly to bring your feet nearest your partner when he approaches you from the direction of your head, it will prove a very useful ability to have in time of need.

You will have also to train for the contingency when the attacker runs around to try evading the defensive screen of your feet. After this you will have to train in suddenly reversing your rotating movement to prepare for the attacker who suddenly changes his direction of circular movement.

In spite of careful training it cannot be ruled out that the attacker may evade your feet and close to the side of your legs. If this should happen you must quickly bend the leg nearest him and bring the elbow of the corresponding arm into close contact with the knee. This affords momentary protection for your side and prevents him coming to grips with your upper body. You should then move sharply away from him by thrusting with your hips in order to bring your feet into play against him once again.

I must stress the importance of learning the protective measures just described. All the knowledge at your disposal of fighting in the standing position is of no use if you cannot protect yourself, however momentarily, if you are thrown, knocked or otherwise fall to the ground during the course of an attack.

It cannot be denied logically that a standing attacker has a great advantage over you when you are in the supine position. While this is true to a great extent you still have one main advantage over the standing attacker. He has to support his weight on one or both of his legs; whereas both of your legs are free from this encumbrance. You are able, therefore, to use either, or both legs to kick him.

You should try out your kicking actions against your partner. As he is constrained to advance one leg in front of the other, in order efficiently to close with you, aim supposedly to bring the sole of one of your feet against the knee which is nearest to you. The kicking action best used is similar to the action required to perform Side Thrust Kick (*peen yonk keok tek*).

Ask your partner to advance his right leg close to your

feet. Twist yourself onto your left side, so that the left side of your body is mainly in contact with the ground, then bend your right leg well, before flexing your leg so that you could dash the sole of your right foot against your partner's right knee.

After some time spent in training when using your right leg with which to implement the kicking action, you could advantageously switch to using the sole of your left foot for the pretence of kicking the advanced knee of your partner.

Once you have acquired a useful knowledge of the movement required to deliver a kick to either of your partner's knees you should try out similar kicking actions delivered towards the middle of your partner's body. This is for the occasion where the over-confident attacker, in a moment of carelessness, leans forward over you.

Another facet of counter-attack from the supine position is to trip the standing attacker to the ground. This would provide you with the opportunity safely to regain your feet. Here are two effective methods of tripping the attacker that gives you a brief respite in which you can safely stand up.

Your partner is presumed to be standing with his right foot in advance while you are lying partially on your back and right side with your feet near to him. Surreptitiously pass your right foot forward closely past the outside of his right ankle then turn your right foot inwards so that the instep of your right foot is positioned close to, but not in contact with, the back of his ankle and your toes point to your right. Partially bend your left leg then turn your left foot inwards so that the toes of your foot point to your right. Gently push the sole of your left foot into the front of your partner's right knee, and slowly bend your right leg so that the instep of your right foot firmly contacts the back of his ankle (*Figure 82*). Continue the contrary movement of your legs to trip your partner gently backwards to the ground.

After you have entrapped his right leg many times with your feet, transpose your tripping actions when your partner advances his left foot.

You will find it rather difficult at first to trip your partner, because of the lack of dexterity possessed by your feet and legs, but after some training this hindrance will largely disappear. At the final stage in training the object is to 'catch' your partner's advanced leg while he is in the act

Figure 82

of transferring his weight from or to his other leg and his foot has not gained too much purchase upon the ground. Take great care that you do not unintentionally hurt your partner, because the feet are not as sensitive as the hands, of course, and therefore at the beginning of training you are apt to misjudge the pressure being applied.

Now try out this alternative technique with your partner when he is standing with both of his legs close by your feet while you are lying partially on your back. Slide both of your feet unobtrusively between his lower legs and then suddenly sit up with outstretched palms held in front of you. Twist your feet outwards so that the insteps of your feet are brought into contact with the back of your partner's ankles then jab the palms of your hands against his knee-caps. These actions will cause your partner slowly to topple over backwards and you can assist your actions by bending your legs so that your feet press against the backs of his ankles.

When one suddenly takes the initiative, from a seemingly particularly weak position, it can prove to be most disconcerting for the attacker, who mistakenly reckons himself to be in an unassailable position.

After you have presumably dealt the attacker an effective blow, or tripped him you are afforded the opportunity to regain your feet. It is imperative that you remember not to get up towards the attacker as otherwise he could possibly still hit or kick you while you are in the process of rising to your feet. The safest way to resume the standing position, in these circumstances, is to bend your right leg well and bring it underneath your body as you support the majority of your weight by resting your right forearm and hand on the ground, by your right side. You continue by planting your left foot on the ground close to your seat and then use the lower part of your right arm and left foot to raise yourself from the surface into a crouching position. You then plant your right foot on the ground before continuing to move away from him as you gradually stand upright at some three yards' distance from him.

Reverse your moves where necessary so that your lower left arm is initially used as a prop for you safely to raise yourself from the ground by moving away from the imagined attacker. Keep practising this recommended way of regaining your feet until you become suitably quick in your actions.